Lee Bailey's
New Orleans

~ ~ ~

Lee Bailey's
New Orleans
Good Food and Glorious Houses

❧ ❧ ❧

by
Lee Bailey
with
Ella Brennan

Recipes from
Commander's Palace, Mr. B's, and The Palace Café

Photographs by
Langdon Clay

Recipe Testing and Development with
Lee Klein

Clarkson Potter/Publishers
New York

For Carol Southern,
a gentle presence, always willing to offer her hand

Design by
DONNA AGAJANIAN

Text copyright © 1993 by Lee Bailey
Photographs copyright ©1993 by Langdon Clay

Published by Clarkson Potter/Publishers, 201 East 50th Street, New York, New York, 10022. Member of the Crown Publishing Group.
Random House, Inc. New York, Toronto, London, Sydney, Auckland

CLARKSON N. POTTER, POTTER and colophon are trademarks of Clarkson N. Potter, Inc.
Manufactured in Japan
Library of Congress Cataloging-in-Publication Data
Bailey, Lee
[New Orleans]
Lee Bailey's New Orleans: good food and glorious houses / by Lee Bailey with Ella Brennan; recipes from Commander's Palace, Mr. B's, and the Palace Café; photographs by Langdon Clay; recipe testing and development with Lee Klein.
p. cm.
includes index
1. Cookery, American—Louisiana style. 2. Cookery—Louisiana—New Orleans. 3. New Orleans (La.)—Description and travel.
I. Brennan, Ella. II. Commander's Palace (Restaurant. III) Mr. B's (Restaurant) IV. Palace Café. V. Title. VI. Title: New Orleans
TX715.2.L68B35 1993
641.59763—dc20   92-31647
CIP
ISBN 0-517-58603-7
10 9 8 7 6 5 4 3 2 1
First Edition

ACKNOWLEDGMENTS

First, to all the gracious people who so generously opened their houses to us, in alphabetical order:

Mr. and Mrs. Jack Aaron, Mr. and Mrs. John Baus, Mr. and Mrs. Joseph DeSilvo, Mr. William Fagaly, Mr. and Mrs. Thomas Favrot, Mr. and Mrs. Walter C. Flower III, Mr. and Mrs. John A. Lynott, Dr. Rise Ochsner, Mr. and Mrs. William Boatner Reily III, Mr. and Mrs. Gus Reynoir, Ms. Ann Rice, Mrs. Sharon Simons, Mr. and Mrs. Rodney Smith, Mrs. Frank Strachan, Mrs. Harold Stream, Dr. and Mrs. Roger Tutton, Mr. and Mrs. Thomas D. Westfeldt II, Mr. and Mrs. Thomas Parker Westervelt, and Mr. and Mrs. Hunter White.

Thanks to the Historic New Orleans Collection and the Pitot House Historic Foundation.

A very special thank you to Leonard Parrish, one of my oldest friends in New Orleans, who was so helpful in getting this project under way. I don't know what we would have done without you!

And to Grover Mouton, who took time out from his busy schedule to track down houses and make suggestions, many thanks.

To Shirley Ratterree, on general principles — and to Patricia Strachan.

To Peggy Gershuny, of the Historic New Orleans Collection, for advice and much help.

At Pitot House, Myrna B. Bergeron, a rare and wonderfully helpful curator, and to Elizabeth Wolf.

At Audubon Park, thanks to Sarah Shirling.

Then, at Commander's Palace Restaurant, my thanks and affection to Ella, Dottie, Dick, and John Brennan — and to chef Jamie Shannon, Mark Holly, Tracy Tonning, Mark Zink, Paul Haylon, Gerard Gravais, Steve Brown, Tim Howard, Clint Stanfield,

Aaron Smith, John Troy, Mark Mancuso, Phil Landry, all the folks in the office, and George.

At Mr. B's Restaurant, many thanks to Ralph and Cindy Brennan, chef Gerard Maras, Gus Martin, Toby Dobson, Randy Sprinkle, Thomas Wolfe, Buzz McGuire, Mary Tell, and Michael Kavanaugh.

At The Palace Café, many thanks to Ti Adelaide Martin, Dick Brennan, Jr., Bradford Bridgeman, and Mary Krepps.

And thanks to Samuel Wilson, Jr., for his telephone comments.

Also, in no particular order, to Rip Naquin and Marty Greenson for letting us photograph from their balcony, George Gibson, John Ordoyne, Darles Leon, Earline Stallworth, Bennie Trehan, Janie Washington, Leslie Stidd, Dee Dillman, Katherine Dillon, Minnie Butler, Sue Quiroz, Audrey Williams, Connie Jones, Alvin Harvey, Caldonia Gaskin, Margie Landry, and finally to Tommy Vandevelde of Tommy's Flower Mart, and Julie.

Now, for these truly gorgeous pictures, my appreciation to Langdon Clay, one of the best, fastest, most unflappable, and energetic photographers I've ever had the fun of working with. It was a pleasure.

And as always, to my old friend and cohort, Lee Klein, who does all the coordinating on these projects — and enough worrying for the lot of us—thanks again.

To the home team at Clarkson Potter, just keep doing what you are doing! Same to my buddy Pam Bernstein.

And to Ellen Violett for suggesting the name of this book, and who, on a visit to New Orleans while we were all working on the project, one evening uttered that magic phrase: "Hey, what about ——— ?"

CONTENTS

INTRODUCTION

New Orleans is jazz, easy livin', the blues — and "When the Saints Come Marchin' In." It's Bourbon Street, St. Charles Avenue, and a street called Desire. It's the ghosts of Satchmo, Lillian Hellman, and Tennessee Williams. It's Mardi Gras, strippers, strong coffee, bars that never close, live oaks, and magnolias. It's uptown society and downtown artists.

But then New Orleans is also terrific food and classic houses. And that's what this book is about — really wonderful food as it is evolving in this truly magical city and the equally marvelous houses you see at every turn.

Although I was born on the Atchafalaya River just about a hundred miles to the north, I didn't get to New Orleans until I finished college in the early 50s. What a great place it was to be young and footloose! And one of the first, best things that happened to me was meeting Ella Brennan. We were the same age and I was trying to get into the design business while she was busy working with her brother Owen to make the legendary old Brennan's on Bourbon Street into one of the hottest places in town — this in a town with no shortage of hot places. Owen was a born showman and restaurateur, and Ella was right in there with him. On weekends we'd all go to the restaurant at seven in the evening and come waltzing out hours later to find a place for a nightcap. Thank heavens I was a kid with stamina.

Okay, about the food. It's no secret that the passing years have changed Crescent City cooking, much as they've changed cooking in every other city around the country. But one of the big differences is that New Orleans had such a rich tradition to build on in the first place. Of course, there are still spots that serve the traditional old food of the city, but frankly when I visit such places today it is more out of sentiment and a hankering for one or two old classics — turtle soup, oyster loaf, gumbo, or bread pudding — than a taste for their general menus. What I enjoy more now is usually less complicated and rich. I suppose my palate has changed along with the times.

So here we have a sampling of what's going on nowadays. New built on the old. Dishes and menus and wine suggestions that Ella and the Brennan clan believe fit the current mood. As in most everything, I couldn't agree more with Miss Ella. The recipes were created by the Brennans' battery of talented young chefs who reign over the kitchens of the Commander's Palace in the Garden District and Mr. B's in the old French Quarter, with a few tasty selections from their new kid on the block, the Palace Café on Canal Street.

This is wonderful food we can all cook and enjoy. For the most part it has been simplified, but it's always stylish, and best of all, delicious.

Now, no one is crazy enough to believe New Orleans cooking is calorie- and fat-free. To tell you the truth, neither of those worthy considerations is of primary concern when I first put together menus. This isn't because I think these factors are unimportant; it's just that I go about the process in a different way — I put together the menus and *then* I think about the calories or fat. Look, I figure by this time, we all know enough about what is healthful and nutritious to make our own decisions and changes — like substituting rice cooked in chicken stock for buttery mashed potatoes, or simply going easy on the sauce that accompanies the main course. I'm not going to tell you what *not* to eat; that's up to you. Who knows, maybe you'd rather have the mashed potatoes and do without something else. Or maybe it's a special occasion and you say, "To hell with it."

We all do it differently. For instance, in almost all cases I substitute low-fat milk for the regular kind when I try new recipes, and I find many instances when evaporated skim milk can take the place of cream. Ditto egg substitutes for whole eggs. And for years I've been using a blend of butter and margarine instead of pure butter. You soon learn when these work and when substitutes compromise the flavor and texture of what you're preparing.

Although I don't go out of my way to do it, I do like to suggest methods that conform to current notions of healthy food preparation where I can. One example is the smoked fish cakes on page 109. They do include a little mayonnaise, but they're baked, not fried — not diet food to be sure, but a sensible alternative. And the vegetable lasagna that accompanies the pompano on page 112 could easily be lifted out of the menu and be made the centerpiece of a fine little vegetable lunch.

Whoever said "Moderation in all things" was a man after my own palate — and mind.

However, there is one category where I take no prisoners — and that is dessert. Desserts should be sweet, and the ones in New Orleans certainly are. I say dessert is something you have in its blissfully seductive form or you skip it. But I don't compromise. That's merely personal — and I do skip desserts or the accompanying whipped cream from time to time. If you are looking for low-cal desserts, look elsewhere. There are always occasions when you want to kick over the traces, and I'm right here, ready to help you do the kicking with my little cloven hoof.

What to say about the houses? Well, unlike the food, the fact that so many of them are basically unchanged, on the outside at least, is what makes these glorious buildings such a pleasure to look at and contemplate. Wandering around the city is like taking a painless course in nineteenth-century southern architectural styles and tastes.

Come on, let's wander — and taste some super food. As they like to say in this city "that care forgot": "Let the good times roll."

Lee Bailey
In the Crescent City

Down below Canal Street everything is different from uptown. Streets are narrow and crowded. Balconies, not trees, shade the walks. Something is going on here. Something is *always* going on here — not quite sinister, but not quite kosher. It's a terrific, exciting place, and parts of it seem never to sleep. Lots of bars, restaurants, music, and exotic

T O W N

entertainment. And lots of people in holiday gear wandering around, trying to puzzle things out — with cameras and maps at the ready. ∾ There's no shortage of places rich in history — like the old St. Louis Cathedral, the Cabildo, and a fine big square named after Andrew Jackson, with a view just over the embankment of the Mississippi River, rolling, rolling. Then there's the French Market, and street musicians, and artists aplenty. ∾ Deeper into the "Quarter," people still live quiet lives and go about their business unruffled by alien visitors that pour in and over the place. Then beyond broad Esplanade Avenue, which marks the back boundary of the Vieux Carré, the city mixes old and new, run-down and built-up. And if you turn and go out Esplanade to its end, you come to another grand park, City Park, and a museum, Delgado, and more history — Bayou St. John. ∾ Except for the park, none of this is like uptown in the least. But all of it is like New Orleans.

Opposite: *Iron fence detail.* **Above:** *The cathedral at Jackson Square.*

This is one of those meals that seafood lovers all know how to handle — literally. It starts pristinely enough with catfish "fingers" that can be offered as a first course at the table or as an hors d'oeuvre with drinks. Actually, this catfish is so good you could make it the whole meal sometime. All you'd need is a salad, or if you want to be traditional, a

A GULF AND RIVER FISH LUNCH

Badia-Fagaly House

Catfish Fingers with Tomato
Tartar Sauce

Barbecued Shrimp and
Cappellini with Shrimp Sauce

Pecan Pie

Rutherford Hill 1987 Gewürtztraminer,
Napa J. Lohr 1990 Gamay Noir,
Monterey

Above: *Barbecued Shrimp and Cappellini with Shrimp Sauce.* **Opposite:** *Courtyard banister.*

salad and fried potatoes. Incidentally, the next time you fry potatoes, leave the skins on. I love them that way. ✸ I seem to have wandered. The *pièce de résistance* here is spicy barbecued whole shrimp. This *is* the way they should be served and, to lots of people, "hands on" is part of the fun. But beware. They can be a mess to peel at the table, so be prepared with plenty of damp napkins. ✸ For this meal, the highly flavored sauce is tossed with pasta to be eaten along with the shrimp. And finally — since we are in a kinda funky, rustic mood — how about pecan pie for dessert? ✸ Beer is often the drink of choice with this combination, but wine is always certainly welcome and so is iced tea. Maybe you should have all three handy. ✸ Now, if you think your crowd is not the kind who wants to *get into* their meal, prepare the shrimp as the recipe calls for, then peel them in the kitchen. Discard the heads and shells and quickly reheat the tails in the sauce.

Catfish Fingers
with Tomato Tartar Sauce

*Of course, if you prefer you could substitute your
favorite tartar sauce for the one here.*

1½ pounds catfish fillets
3 tablespoons Creole mustard (see Note, page 87)
2 tablespoons dry white wine
½ teaspoon salt
¼ teaspoon black pepper
Peanut oil for frying
1 cup yellow cornmeal
½ cup corn flour
⅓ cup cornstarch
1 tablespoon Creole Seasoning (page 109)

Cut catfish fillets into ½- by 2-inch strips. Combine
the mustard, wine, salt, and pepper. Add the catfish
strips and toss to coat well. Cover and marinate for
an hour.

Heat oil in a deep fryer to 350 degrees.

Mix together the cornmeal, corn flour, cornstarch
and Creole Seasoning. Spread out on a sheet of
waxed paper. Roll the marinated strips in the
mixture, lightly shaking off any excess. Fry until
golden, about 4 minutes. Drain on paper towels and
serve with Tomato Tartar Sauce (recipe follows).

Serves 6

Tomato Tartar Sauce
1 cup pureed peeled and seeded fresh tomato
  (or the same amount of canned)
1 cup dry white wine
½ cup tomato juice
1 teaspoon minced garlic
2½ cups mayonnaise
¼ cup minced white onion
¼ cup drained sweet pickle relish
1 tablespoon minced fresh tarragon
½ teaspoon Louisiana Hot Sauce
½ teaspoon salt
Whites of 2 hard-cooked eggs, minced

Combine the tomato puree, wine, tomato juice, and
garlic in a small saucepan and bring quickly to a
boil, stirring, over high heat. Turn the heat down to
a simmer and reduce the mixture to 1 cup without
stirring, about 20 to 25 minutes. Allow to cool.

Add the cooled tomato reduction to the
mayonnaise, onion, and relish in a food processor.
Puree and scrape out into a bowl. Mix in all other
ingredients, correct seasoning if necessary, and chill.

Makes about 3 cups

Above: *Fanlit doorway.*

Above: *Catfish Fingers with Tomato Tartar Sauce.* **Below:** *An eclectic collection of art on the mantel.*

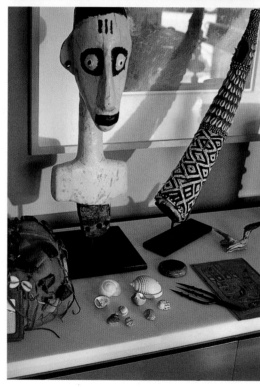

Top: *Patio balcony.* Above: *African art.* Right: *Lily on the patio.* Opposite: *Badia-Fagaly House.*

ABOUT THE HOUSE

The meager historical records don't say much about the Spanish Colonial house, but they do help us learn about the original owner. It's a poignant story.

"The house was built by Jayme Badia, a white man, for his illegitimate *quadroon* daughter, Rosalie, who was mothered by a *mulatto,* Rosette Rachon" (the stress is mine). These unpleasant distinctions of color were commonplace in both the law and everyday conversation during the eighteenth and nineteenth centuries here — and they persisted well into the second half of this century. Whatever the circumstances (legitimacy was legally out of the question), Badia obviously cared enough about his daughter's and her mother's well-being to provide shelter for them.

As to the house itself, stylistic and factual information about similar houses in the Quarter would lead one to conclude it was built between 1763 and 1803. The house was originally two separate buildings — a *boulangerie* (baker's shop) or *boucherie* (butcher shop) and living quarters in the front building, and a kitchen and *garçonnière* (bachelor's quarters) in the rear. A telling architectural feature is the exterior staircase in the courtyard. This provides us with another strong clue for the building's original date: During 1763 to 1803 (the period when the city was under Spanish rule) the law calculated and set property taxes by — among other things — the number of interior staircases and closets in a building. This was often circumvented by putting the staircases outside and substituting armoires for closets.

While the house might not have a specific date, it does have a specific style.

Above: *At table, with a centerpiece of Mexican* papier-mâché *fruit and vegetables.* **Below:** *Pecan Pie.*

Barbecued Shrimp and Cappellini with Shrimp Sauce

To do this right, plan to cook the shrimp in batches. Even that way, it doesn't take too long.

3½ to 4 pounds large shrimp in their shells with heads on
4½ teaspoons ground black pepper
4½ teaspoons cracked black pepper
1 tablespoon Creole Seasoning (page 109)
9 tablespoons Homemade Worcestershire Sauce (page 140)
1 tablespoon minced garlic
1 cup (2 sticks) unsalted butter
Juice of 3 lemons
3 tablespoons water
8 ounces cappellini

Preheat oven to 450 degrees.

Place half the shrimp in a large, heavy ovenproof skillet, about 12 inches (they should fit in a single layer). Sprinkle with *half* the peppers, Creole Seasoning, Worcestershire Sauce, and garlic. Dot with half a stick of the butter. Place in the oven. Cook for 2 minutes, turn, and cook for another 2 minutes. Remove to the top of the stove and continue to cook for another 4 minutes, tossing lightly, over medium-high heat. Off the heat, stir in the juice of 1½ lemons and 1 tablespoon plus 1½ teaspoons of the water. Then stir in the other half stick of butter, cut into pieces. When butter is melted, lift the shrimp out with a slotted spoon into a large bowl, cover with a tea towel to keep warm, and pour sauce into a small saucepan.

Repeat with the remaining shrimp and other ingredients.

To serve, cook pasta in lightly salted water until al dente. Reheat the sauce and lightly coat the shrimp with it. Toss pasta with a bit of the sauce and serve the balance of the sauce on the side.

Serves 6

Pecan Pie

The marvelous old classic revisited.

Pastry

1¾ cups flour
½ cup sugar
¼ teaspoon salt
½ teaspoon baking powder
½ teaspoon nutmeg
1 teaspoon cinnamon
½ cup (1 stick) unsalted butter, cut into pieces
1 egg lightly beaten

Filling

1 cup light corn syrup
1 cup sugar
½ cup (1 stick) unsalted butter, melted
4 eggs
½ teaspoon vanilla extract
1 cup coarsely chopped pecans

Make the pastry: Place all ingredients, except the egg, in a food processor and pulse until mixture is the texture of coarse meal. Add the egg and pulse until dough just begins to cling together. Gather into a ball, wrap, flattening slightly, and refrigerate for about 1 hour.

Roll out dough between 2 sheets of waxed paper into about a 10-inch circle, ⅛ inch thick. Line an 8-inch pie pan with it and crimp the edges.

Complete the pie: Preheat oven to 350 degrees.

In a large bowl, mix syrup and sugar at low speed for about 2 minutes to dissolve sugar. Beat in butter, eggs, and vanilla briefly. Mix in pecans and pour into prepared crust.

Bake until set, about 45 to 55 minutes.

Cool and serve plain or topped with some whipped cream or ice cream.

Serves 8

SPRING LUNCH

Dolliole-Lynott House

Oyster Shooters

Shrimp *Maque Choux* Salad

Corn Muffins and New Orleans French Bread

Rocky Road Squares with Caramel Sauce

Alsace Pinot Gris "Reserve" Trimbach 1984

What a good menu this is for a balmy spring lunch on the patio! Oyster shooters start the occasion off on the right foot; the twist on shrimp salad is as much a treat for the palate as it is to the eyes. Then there's both New Orleans French bread and corn muffins to go along with the salad. This is as good a place as any to tell you about New Orleans French bread. It is like no other I've ever tasted — light as a feather and perfect toasted. I've included a recipe for it contributed by friends at the G. H. Leidenheimer Baking Company. ⌒ Since you've been more or less minding your calories, one of those temptingly sinful concoctions follows. Rocky road squares with caramel sauce — in case you're in the mood to fall off the wagon. Of course you could skip it or settle for a couple of strawberries. Dealer's choice.

Opposite: *Cast iron bench.*

Above: *Oyster Shooters.* **Below:** *The old slave quarters.*

Oyster Shooters

New Orleans is a hard-drinking, fun-loving town, and sometimes even innocent little bivalves are named after a drink. Serve these raw oysters in anything the size of a shot glass, with their sauce, to be tossed back like a shot of bourbon. Unlike bourbon, though, you can serve 4 to 6 of these per person.

The sauce here is a typical rather mayonnaisey mixture, but you could certainly substitute whatever sauce you might like.

3 egg yolks
1 cup olive oil
Juice of 1 lemon
2 teaspoons Worcestershire Sauce
2 tablespoons red wine vinegar
2 tablespoons minced shallots
2 tablespoons coarsely ground black pepper
Salt to taste
24 to 36 shucked oysters
3 lemons, quartered, for garnish

Put the yolks in a small bowl and drizzle olive oil over them while whisking. When all the oil is incorporated, whisk in the lemon juice and Worcestershire Sauce. Stir in vinegar, shallots, pepper, and salt. Mix well.

To serve, place a bit of sauce in each of 24 to 36 shot glasses, then put an oyster in each. Top with more sauce. Serve with lemon quarters and extra sauce on the side, if desired.

Serves 6

Shrimp *Maque Choux* Salad

There is a popular traditional corn and tomato salad in the Deep South called maque choux. *The version here has some wonderfully spicy shrimp added. By itself, it would be a light and tasty luncheon dish.*

1 quart cold water
½ large lemon, cut in two
6 tablespoons salt
¼ cup Louisiana Hot Sauce
1½ teaspoons cayenne pepper
2 tablespoons minced garlic
2¼ pounds shrimp with their heads on
¼ cup olive oil
2 large green bell peppers, diced finely
2 large red bell peppers, diced finely
Kernels from 3 ears of corn
1 medium red onion, diced finely
2 tablespoons minced cilantro (optional)
Salt to taste
1 teaspoon white pepper, or to taste
Juice of 1 large lime
Bibb lettuce and radicchio leaves

Place water in a large, deep pot. Squeeze the lemon juice into it, and add the squeezed lemon. Add the salt, hot sauce, cayenne, and garlic and bring to a boil over high heat. Add the shrimp and cook for 1 minute. Allow shrimp to cool slightly in the boil, then drain and peel. Set aside.

Heat olive oil in a deep skillet over a medium-high flame and sauté peppers, corn, and onion until just wilted, about 5 minutes. Do not brown. Stir in cilantro, salt, and pepper, then add the lime juice. Mix. Add shrimp and toss.

Serve on Bibb lettuce and radicchio leaves.

Serves 6

ABOUT THE HOUSE

As early as 1779, this parcel of land was owned by a family of freed slaves. It stood vacant until the 1830s when Jean Louis Dolliole — who headed the family — built a typical French Quarter Creole cottage. He and his brothers were first-rate carpenters and were responsible for erecting many similar houses.

The plan was simplicity itself: two rooms in front and two in back, each with its own fireplace. The sharply pitched roof was punctuated with dormers; four bays marked a facade that opened directly onto the street. There was little concern paid to such "amenities" as ventilation or natural light.

The backs of the houses almost always gave onto an open patio, as this one does, with two-story slave quarters one-room deep.

When the first major renovation was begun here in the 1960s, there were dirt floors and no indoor plumbing. A new floor was made with bricks from the original chimney. Large French doors, with arched fanlights and sidelights, were added to replace narrow ones. These new doors make it possible to open the entire back of the house onto the patio.

Similar reconstruction was done on the back building to provide extra bedrooms and baths. Once again bricks that had tumbled out from the collapsed fireplaces were used to replace dirt floors and build new fireplaces.

Similar renovations are being undertaken throughout the French Quarter these days, aided by and watched over by the Vieux Carré Commission, ensuring that many of these charming simple houses, which have contributed so much to the particular character of the neighborhood, will continue to have a vital existence well into the next century.

Corn Muffins

1 tablespoon vegetable oil
¾ cup all-purpose flour
1¼ cups yellow cornmeal
2 tablespoons sugar
2 teaspoons baking powder
1 teaspoon salt
1 cup milk
4 tablespoons (½ stick) unsalted butter, melted
1 egg, beaten

Preheat oven to 375 degrees. Liberally spray a
12-muffin tin with vegetable-oil spray, then put
¼ teaspoon of the vegetable oil in each tin. Place in
the oven while you mix the batter quickly.

Sift all the dry ingredients together and stir to mix.
Combine all the liquid ingredients and mix well.
Pour the wet into the dry mixture and stir lightly —
do not overmix. Spoon the batter into the prepared
heated cups to about three-quarters full.

Bake until just turning golden, about 20 to 25
minutes.

Makes 12 muffins

Opposite: *Upstairs balcony of the guesthouse.* **Above,
from top:** *Shrimp Maque Choux Salad,
Corn Muffins, and New Orleans French Bread on
the table. Patio water lily. Watercolor of Dolliole-
Lynott House.*

Above: *Guest room chair.* **Above right:** *Hibiscus in bloom.* **Below:** *Rocky Road Squares with Caramel Sauce.*

New Orleans French Bread

Here it is, folks — a proven winner!
Special thanks to the folks at the G. H. Leidenheimer
Baking Company for this recipe.

2 cups warm (110 degrees) water
2 tablespoons sugar
2 tablespoons dry granulated yeast
2 tablespoons vegetable shortening
6½ cups bread flour
1 tablespoon salt

Place the 2 cups water in the bowl of a stationary mixer fitted with a dough hook. Add 1 tablespoon sugar and sprinkle with the yeast. Allow to sit for about 15 minutes, until the mixture is bubbling. Add the remaining 1 tablespoon of sugar, the shortening, and 5 cups of flour. Mix until a dough starts to form. Add the salt and the remaining flour as needed until the dough forms a ball and pulls away from the sides of the bowl. Continue to knead with the dough hook for 10 minutes.

Turn the dough out onto a lightly floured board and knead by hand for a minute or two, until dough is smooth and elastic. Return it to the mixing bowl, cover with plastic wrap, and set in a warm, draft-free corner to rise for 1½ hours, or until doubled in size.

Punch the dough down, then divide it into four balls. Cover these with a clean dishtowel and let them rest for 15 minutes. Form each ball into a 16 x 3-inch loaf. Place the loaves on baking sheets, cover them with a damp cloth, and set aside to rise for 1½ hours.

Preheat oven to 375 degrees.

Gently place the fully risen loaves in the preheated oven and bake for about 30 minutes, until golden brown. Cool on racks.

Makes 4 loaves

Rocky Road Squares with Caramel Sauce

Not only does this adult version of a kid's
dessert tickle your palate, it may be made in advance
and stored in the freezer for months.

10 ounces semisweet chocolate, chopped
3 tablespoons unsalted butter
3 egg yolks
¼ cup sugar
4 egg whites
2½ cups chopped pecans, toasted
4 ounces mini marshmallows

Caramel Sauce (page 143)

Melt the chocolate and set it aside. Whip the butter until light and fluffy. Beat in the melted chocolate. Whip the egg yolks with half the sugar until light yellow. Set aside. Whip egg whites with the other half of the sugar until soft peaks form. Fold yolk mixture into the chocolate-butter mixture, then fold in the egg whites. Lastly fold in the pecans and marshmallows.

Open the top end of a 1-quart paper milk carton completely. Rinse it out and dry it. Spoon mixture into carton, shaking it down lightly, until carton is filled. Cover and place in the freezer.

To serve, rip the carton off and cut slices with a knife dipped into hot water and dried. Serve with Caramel Sauce or pureed strawberries.

Serves 6 to 8

Note: You may also make this in a buttered 1-quart terrine. The milk carton doesn't need buttering.

SUPPER IN THE LIBRARY

LaBlanche-DeSalvo-James House

Warm Grilled Mushroom Salad with
Rice Vinaigrette

Wasabi Crust Baked Salmon Fillet with Orange
Anaheim Pepper Sauce

Basic Broccoli

Buttered Potatoes

White Chocolate Brownie with Chocolate Sauce
and Vanilla Ice Cream

Chablis Premier Cru "Vallions" Servin 1989

When I lived in New Orleans years ago, fresh salmon was almost never served. And because I didn't grow up eating salmon — like I did redfish, perch, catfish, and trout — I didn't know what I was missing. I soon made up for lost time, and now I like salmon prepared almost any way. So if you share my taste you will be delighted with the recipe in this menu. It has a luscious flavor and it's simple to prepare, with or without the sauce. Accompaniments are broccoli and basic buttered potatoes — simple, but a perfect foil for the distinctive salmon. Now, broccoli, which I would guess to be in every market and on most restaurant menus today, was practically unknown in the hot and humid Deep South until the 40s. ❧ The first course is a warm salad utilizing shiitake mushrooms, another ingredient that was pretty scarce years ago. It may not have become a staple, but it's more or less available. ❧ Not even dessert will break this mood. Our brownies have a "modern" twist — they're made with white chocolate, another rarity thirty years ago. I don't mean these ingredients were unknown, they simply weren't used often. So when someone moons over how terrific things used to be, remember salmon, shiitake mushrooms, broccoli, and white chocolate, and give them the old Gioconda smile.

Left: *Library dining room.* **Opposite:** *Warm Grilled Mushroom Salad with Rice Vinaigrette.*

ABOUT THE HOUSE

In 1925, a young William Faulkner came to New Orleans to catch a tramp steamer to France. Apparently, he fell for the city, because he moved into the LaBlanche-DeSalvo-James House with his friend William Spratling and stayed on to write *Soldier's Pay,* his first novel, as well as pieces for the *Times-Picayune.* And while he was living in this house he met and fell in love with Helen Baird. Is it any wonder that the house is also known as Faulkner House?

The house itself is built on a piece of land that was the site of the old Colonial prison (abandoned by the city in 1830). At some time in the early 1830s it was purchased by Melasie Trepagnier LaBlanche, widow of Jean Baptiste LaBlanche, a wealthy sugar planter from St. Charles Parish. By 1840, or thereabouts, the square had been converted into a group of eleven tall narrow city houses that she, her family, and planter friends occupied.

All these houses had spiral staircases and balconies on every floor; small rear courtyards give onto a "secret" locked alley leading to the Cabildo. Faulkner House's balconies afford a lovely view of the landscaped garden that backs St. Louis Cathedral. Originally, the modest courtyard held another small building and a three-story dependency for servants and sons of the house. These structures were connected to make the single unit that exists today.

In 1988 it was purchased by the present owners, who completely renovated the building, creating an elegant residence. They also provided space for a ground-floor bookstore commemorating the house's illustrious former tenant.

Warm Grilled Mushroom Salad with Rice Vinaigrette

Try this with fresh porcini mushrooms if they're available, or put together a combination of different kinds. P. S. The salad would be a fine little lunch by itself.

18 medium shiitake mushrooms, brushed and wiped
   clean with stems trimmed to ¼ inch
¼ teaspoon salt
¼ teaspoon white pepper
2 tablespoons olive oil
2 small heads red oak leaf lettuce, washed and dried
2 small heads *frisée* lettuce, washed and dried
Rice Vinaigrette (recipe follows)

Preheat grill or broiler.

Place mushrooms in a bowl and sprinkle with half the salt and pepper. Drizzle 1 tablespoon of the oil over all and toss to coat. Grill or broil until just tender, 3 to 4 minutes. Do not overcook. Place in a small warmed metal bowl as they cook and toss with the remaining salt, pepper, and olive oil. Keep warm.

Tear greens into bite-size pieces and toss with the Rice Vinaigrette.

To serve, arrange greens on individual plates and place 3 mushrooms on each, pouring any oil and juice which may have accumulated in the mushroom bowl over each plate.

Serves 6

Rice Vinaigrette
¼ cup olive oil
2 teaspoons rice wine vinegar
Pinch of salt
Pinch of pepper

Whisk all ingredients together.

Wasabi Crust Baked Salmon Fillet with Orange Anaheim Pepper Sauce

This dish could be made lighter by serving the salmon with a salsa flavored with oranges.

1 ounce wasabi (Japanese horseradish)
½ cup water
1½ cups toasted bread crumbs
¼ cup mayonnaise
1 tablespoon honey
¼ teaspoon salt
2 tablespoons sesame seeds
6 4- to 6-ounce salmon fillets, with any remaining
   bones removed
1 tablespoon cold unsalted butter, cut into bits
Orange Anaheim Pepper Sauce (page 34)

Preheat oven to 425 degrees.

Mix wasabi with water to form a paste. Let it rest for 20 minutes. Place all ingredients except salmon, butter, and pepper sauce in a small bowl and combine with your hands to make a moist mixture.

Put several tablespoons of water in a baking sheet to prevent sticking (you want a film of water in the pan) and lay the fillets on it. Pat mixture on top of each fillet to about ¼-inch thickness. Dot with the butter and bake for 6 to 7 minutes. Center of fish should be slightly undercooked.

Serve with Orange Anaheim Pepper Sauce.

Serves 6

Opposite: *Living room corner.*
Right: *Faulkner House.*
Overleaf: *Chair and sofa at opposite sides of the living room.*

Orange Anaheim Pepper Sauce

⅓ cup fresh orange juice
Zest of 2 medium oranges
¼ cup dry white wine
3 tablespoons white wine vinegar
3 tablespoons minced Anaheim pepper, including a
   few seeds
2 tablespoons heavy cream
1 cup (2 sticks) cold unsalted butter, cut into 1-inch pieces
¼ teaspoon salt
Pinch of white pepper

Place juice in a small nonreactive pot with the zest, wine, and vinegar. Reduce over high heat until syrupy, about 10 minutes. Off the heat, add pepper and cream and whisk to combine. Return to a medium flame and whisk in butter a piece at a time until all is incorporated. Sprinkle in salt and pepper, adding more if desired.

Makes about 1⅓ cups

Basic Broccoli

*You could steam the broccoli instead of blanching
it — it holds well either way.*

1 medium head broccoli, florets only
1 tablespoon unsalted butter
½ teaspoon salt
½ teaspoon white pepper

Blanch florets in salted boiling water for 1½ minutes. Immediately immerse in ice water. Drain and reserve. To serve, toss in the butter over medium heat to warm through. Season with the salt and pepper to taste.

Serves 6

Buttered Potatoes

6 medium new potatoes, about 1¼ pounds, peeled
1 tablespoon unsalted butter
½ teaspoon salt
½ teaspoon white pepper

Simmer potatoes in well-salted water until just tender, 10 to 12 minutes. Drain well. To serve, put them in a skillet over medium heat with the butter. Toss and season with the salt and pepper to taste.

Serves 6

White Chocolate Brownie with Chocolate Sauce and Vanilla Ice Cream

You could salve your conscience by leaving off either the chocolate sauce or the ice cream.

7 tablespoons unsalted butter
8 ounces white chocolate, half chopped fine and half chopped coarse
2 eggs
Pinch of salt
½ cup sugar
1½ teaspoons vanilla extract
1 cup flour
4 ounces bittersweet chocolate, chopped coarse
Chocolate Sauce (recipe follows)

Preheat oven to 350 degrees and lightly grease an 8-inch-square baking pan. Line with foil and butter the foil. Set aside.

Melt the butter over low heat in a small heavy saucepan. Sprinkle in the finely chopped white chocolate. Do not stir. Set aside.

With a hand mixer at high speed, beat eggs and salt until frothy. Continue to beat while adding the sugar. Beat for 2 minutes. Stir in the chocolate-butter mixture, vanilla, and flour, mixing until smooth. Fold in the remaining white and the bittersweet chocolate, and spread in the prepared pan.

Bake for 35 minutes. Allow to cool on a rack.

Serve each slice on a slick of chocolate sauce, topped with a scoop of vanilla ice cream.

Serves 9 to 12

Chocolate Sauce

½ cup heavy cream
3 tablespoons unsalted butter, cut into bits
⅓ cup granulated sugar
⅓ cup dark brown sugar
Pinch of salt
½ cup sifted unsweetened cocoa powder
¼ cup strong coffee (optional)

Place cream and butter in a large heavy saucepan and heat over a moderate flame, stirring, until butter melts and cream just begins to boil. Add the sugars and salt and stir to dissolve. Reduce the heat and whisk in the cocoa until smooth. Remove from heat and thin with coffee if necessary.

Makes about ¾ cup

We figured an elegantly restored house deserved an elegant little celebration dinner party. So first are absolutely delicious fried oyster mushrooms with a mayonnaise strongly flavored with rosemary. The main course is broiled medallions of lamb —

A LITTLE CELEBRATION DINNER

Le Baron-Tutton House

Fried Oyster Mushrooms with
Rosemary Mayonnaise

Broiled Lamb Medallions

Sweet Vidalia Onion Sauce

Buttered Carrots and Yellow Peppers
with Parsley

Gaufrette Potatoes

Angel Food Cake with Lemon Sauce
and Raspberries

Caymus "Special Selection" 1988
Côtes de Nuits-Villages, Faiveley 1988

wonderfully easy — sweet Vidalia onion sauce, carrots and yellow peppers tossed with parsley butter. Fresh gaufrette potatoes, which are nothing more than rather glamorized potato chips, give the meal a little crunch. ∽ Finally, the dessert. While angel food cakes were slipping into oblivion elsewhere, they never lost their appeal in the South, where they are still a favorite to serve with ice cream. However, angel food cake and ice cream seemed a little too much like birthday fare so we decided to add lemon sauce and untypical raspberries to the mix.

Above: *Broiled Lamb Medallions with Sweet Vidalia Onion Sauce, Buttered Carrots and Yellow Peppers with Parsley, and Gaufrette Potatoes.* **Opposite:** *Entrance stairway.*

Fried Oyster Mushrooms with Rosemary Mayonnaise

These mushrooms would also be awfully good with any salsa.

1½ cups flour
¼ cup cornstarch
½ teaspoon paprika
¾ teaspoon salt
½ teaspoon black pepper
2 tablespoons minced parsley
2 eggs
1⅓ cups milk
18 unbroken well-shaped oyster mushrooms
Vegetable oil for frying
Rosemary Mayonnaise (recipe follows)

Toss together in a bowl the flour, cornstarch, paprika, salt, pepper, and parsley. Set aside. In another bowl beat together the eggs and milk.

Toss mushrooms in flour, then egg wash, and then back in flour. Deep fry in oil at 365 degrees for about 4 minutes, or until golden. Drain and serve immediately with Rosemary Mayonnaise.

Serves 6

Rosemary Mayonnaise

1¼ cup vegetable oil
¼ cup olive oil
1 tablespoon minced fresh rosemary leaves
1 egg yolk
1 tablespoon water
¼ cup white wine vinegar
¼ cup rice wine vinegar
¼ teaspoon salt
¼ teaspoon white pepper

Slowly heat the oils in a saucepan over a low flame. Remove from heat and stir in rosemary leaves. Allow to rest at room temperature for an hour or more to infuse.

Whisk the egg yolk and water together in a bowl. Strain oils and slowly drizzle over yolk, whisking, until all oil is emulsified. Whisk in the vinegars, salt, and pepper.

Opposite: *Fried Oyster Mushrooms with Rosemary Mayonnaise.*

Broiled Lamb Medallions

The marinade gives the lamb just the right amount of seasoning.

1½ pounds (boned weight) lamb loin
¼ cup Dijon mustard
2 tablespoons fresh rosemary leaves
2 tablespoons dry white wine
2 tablespoons white wine vinegar
1 teaspoon black pepper
1 to 2 tablespoons unsalted butter, melted

Trim all fat from lamb and place in a shallow dish. Mix together all the other ingredients except butter and pour over meat, turning it to make sure all surfaces are well coated. Cover and refrigerate overnight, turning once or twice.

To cook, remove the lamb from the refrigerator at least an hour before you preheat the broiler. Blot off excess marinade. Cut the lamb into 1¼-inch slices and brush the slices with melted butter. Broil about 3 inches from the flame for 2 to 3 minutes per side, brushing with butter as you turn meat.

Serves 6

Sweet Vidalia Onion Sauce

This sauce would be great on pork too.

2 tablespoons unsalted butter
3 cups thin strips Vidalia onions (about 1½ pounds)
½ cup Sauternes (or other sweet wine)
3 cups beef, veal, or lamb stock (or a combination)
1 large bay leaf
½ teaspoon black pepper
Salt to taste

Heat 1 tablespoon of the butter in a large sauté pan. Add onions and cook over medium-high heat, stirring occasionally, until they are caramelized, about 12 to 15 minutes. Add the Sauternes, stock, bay leaf, and black pepper. Continue to cook on medium heat for another 15 minutes to reduce. Whisk in the remaining tablespoon of butter off the heat. Check for salt and serve.

Makes 2 cups

ABOUT THE HOUSE

This classically beautiful house — almost totally obliterated over the years — has been rescued and returned to its original glory, and then some.

The saga began around 1821 when the federal government sold the land to Jacob Brandegee. By 1827 Claude Alexandre Le Baron had apparently purchased the land from Brandegee, and between then and 1836 a house such as the one you see now was erected.

The years between 1825 and 1850 were the go-go years in New Orleans's economic history. Fortunes were amassed and spent, or lost. Such was the case here. Legal action against Le Baron revealed that in 1830 he had given this property to his wife, Anne Malus. In an effort to disassociate the Le Baron House from her husband's other assets, Mme. Le Baron tried to prove the property had come to her "solely as a token of friendship and gratitude toward her" and not as the result of an effort to evade the demands of creditors. Alas, Mme. Le Baron's explanation apparently fell on deaf ears and the whole property

Far left, from top: *Arrowhead in a planter. View through a window. Camellia Sinensis.* Above left: *Le Baron-Tutton House.*
Above: *View of the interior garden.* Overleaf: *The red library.*

was put up for public sale — thereby starting the property's long and ignominious slide to decrepitude. In 1964, Edith Long noted: "This building has been so changed that at first glance it seems commonplace, when in truth, if it were restored to the pattern that can be so clearly read on its facade, it would be a classic type of the buildings of its time."

However, that decline was reversed when its current owners bought the place in 1988. Their only alternative was to start tearing away, making careful notes as

demolition work progressed, to discover the true shape and design of the house when it was first built. This was a painstaking, frustrating, and exciting experience for both the owners and architect John C. Williams, who guided the redesign and reconstruction. Along the way, the garden patio was restored and back and side buildings typical of the period were constructed.

This time around the story has a happy ending.

Buttered Carrots and Yellow Peppers with Parsley

This is a nice contrast of textures — and colors.

4 large carrots, scraped and cut into ½-inch rounds
1 tablespoon unsalted butter
1 medium yellow pepper, seeded and cut into
    medium dice
¼ cup coarsely chopped Italian parsley
¼ teaspoon salt
¼ teaspoon white pepper

Cover carrots with well-salted water and bring to a boil. Turn back to medium and cook until tender, about 10 minutes. Plunge into cold water and drain.

To serve, melt butter in a skillet and toss carrots and yellow pepper together long enough to heat them through, 2 or 3 minutes. Off the heat, stir in parsley, salt, and pepper.

Serves 6

Gaufrette Potatoes

You'll need a mandoline to make the fancy cut pictured on page 36. If you don't have one, simply make thin-sliced potatoes.

¾ to 1 pound baking potatoes, peeled
Oil for deep-frying
Salt

To prepare potatoes, score with the mandoline blade, then turn 90 degrees and slice thin. Drop in cold water.

Preheat oil in deep fryer to 365 degrees.

Dry the potatoes *well* and fry in small batches until golden, about 4 minutes.

Drain on paper towels and sprinkle with salt.

Serves 6

Angel Food Cake with Lemon Sauce and Raspberries

Both the sauce and the cake may be made the day before.

1⅓ cups sugar, sifted 3 times
1 cup all-purpose flour, sifted 5 times
11 egg whites, at room temperature
1 teaspoon salt
1½ teaspoons cream of tartar
1 teaspoon vanilla extract
Lemon Sauce (recipe follows)

Preheat oven to 400 degrees and butter a 10 x 3-inch-deep cake pan. Line bottom of pan with a circle of parchment and butter again. Set aside.

Mix ⅓ cup of the sugar with the flour. Beat egg whites with a hand mixer at medium speed until foamy. Add salt and after about a minute turn mixer to high and add cream of tartar. Beat another few minutes and turn back to medium. Gradually add the remaining sugar, mixing all the while, until mixture makes stiff glossy peaks. Stir in vanilla. Fold in flour-sugar mixture a fourth at a time. Stop when everything is well incorporated. Do not overmix.

Pour and scrape into pan and bake for 8 minutes. Turn heat down to 325 degrees and bake an additional 25 to 35 minutes, until a cake tester comes out clean and the top is light golden. Allow to cool slightly before removing from pan.

Serve topped with Lemon Sauce and raspberries.

Serves 12

Lemon Sauce

1½ teaspoons cornstarch
¾ cup fresh lemon juice
6 tablespoons sugar, or more to taste

Mix cornstarch with the lemon juice in a small saucepan and cook over a low flame, stirring, until mixture thickens slightly, about 1 or 2 minutes. Stir in sugar and continue to cook, stirring, for another 2 to 3 minutes. Serve warm.

Makes about ¾ cup

Above: *Angel Food Cake with Lemon Sauce and Raspberries.* **Below**: *Potpourri.*

A Crescent City Italian Meal

Lombard-Simons House

Grilled Eggplant with Ricotta and
Two Tomatoes

Grilled Veal Chop with Smoked Tomato Sauce

Roasted Potatoes

Sautéed Kohlrabi

Mixed Greens with Champagne Vinaigrette

Chocolate Mousse Cake

Duckhorn Cabernet Sauvignon Napa 1988
Châteauneuf-du-Pape, Chateau de Beaucastel
1988

Now here we have a rather un-New Orleans menu. Only the slightest hint of Crescent City roots shows in the smoked tomatoes used in a sauce for grilled veal chops. You know all good ol' boys have smokers, but did you ever hear of smoking tomatoes? Well, you're in for a treat. The other typical New Orleans aspect to the menu is the cake for dessert. Not the *particular* cake, mind, but the fact that cake finishes the meal. Cakes seem to have remained more popular here than in other parts of the country. But back to the beginning. ᴄ The meal starts with grilled eggplant and fresh ricotta topped by a combination of fresh and sun-dried tomatoes. Italian to the core. There's always been an Italian influence — mostly Neapolitan — in New Orleans, but lately a more varied influence is beginning to show itself in earnest. It'll be fun to see what comes of this marriage between Northern Italian tastes and all that New Orleans culinary jazz. Crawfish ravioli, anyone? ᴄ By the second course we have managed to have tomatoes three different ways: uncooked, sun-dried, and smoked. That's what I call a little bit of heaven. Food purists might consider this too much of a good thing, but not here. Natives cherish tomatoes second only to seafood. To go with the veal are simple roasted potatoes. We pause for a little salad and then on to the marvelously moist chocolate cake.

Opposite: *Entrance door.*

Above: *Garden dining room table.* **Below:** *Patio treillage.*

Above: *Hydrangeas.* Below: *Living room chaise.*

Grilled Eggplant with Ricotta and Two Tomatoes

Make this a small course; there's lots more to come. This is very good served warm if you can manage it. If not, it works fine at room temperature.

12 to 18 ¼-inch slices of unpeeled eggplant
1 teaspoon salt
6 to 7 tablespoons olive oil
1 ounce sun-dried tomatoes, cut into thin strips
2 medium tomatoes, peeled
¼ teaspoon black pepper
1 tablespoon minced fresh oregano
6 tablespoons fresh ricotta cheese
6 medium green onions, cut into thin rings including
    some green

Preheat the grill or oven broiler. Place eggplant slices on a flat pan and sprinkle with ½ teaspoon salt. Drizzle 2 or 3 tablespoons olive oil over them and turn to coat slices with oil. Set aside for at least 5 minutes.

Cover sun-dried tomatoes with hot water and set them aside.

Quarter the peeled tomatoes, and remove and discard the seeds and watery pulp. Cut the flesh into a medium julienne. Put in a bowl. Drain and dry the sun-dried tomatoes, add to the fresh tomato with the remaining olive oil and ½ teaspoon of salt. Stir in oregano. Set aside.

Grill eggplant slices until golden on both sides, 4 to 5 minutes, turning several times. Keep warm.

To assemble, place a tablespoon of ricotta in the center of 6 small plates. Divide grilled eggplant among the plates, arranging the slices over the cheese. Spoon tomato topping over each and sprinkle with green onions.

Serves 6

ABOUT THE HOUSE

The anecdotal information that can cling to a piece of property can be both amusing and puzzling. Take the Lombard-Simons House. There's nothing about noble gestures, brave fights, terrible reversals, or illustrious ancestors, but rather a persistent rumor that in the 1930s the place was a brothel. I suppose that's not surprising in the city "that care forgot" — especially in the French Quarter. Anyway, the rumor can be traced.

The house was purchased in 1937 by Gertrude Hoffmire Dix Anderson. Gertrude was the widow of Tom Anderson, infamous "mayor" of infamous Storyville, New Orleans's infamous red-light district. People who should have known said she was a madam reputed to possess the obligatory heart of gold, a lively intelligence, and charm. I see a young Claire Trevor in the part. Whatever the truth of any of this, Gertrude apparently went to work for Tom around 1909, and was an exceptional businesswoman. In 1917, when the U.S. Navy was ordered to close Storyville, Gertrude actually went to court to stop the closure, basing her case on the contention that the government was hampering

free enterprise. She lost the case. In 1928, Gertrude and Tom married — he was seventy-one and she well into her fifties. By all accounts, the bride was a respected and respectable old lady when she died here in her eighties.

Most everything else we know is pretty dry, but here's some of it. On October 6, 1786, the Community of the Ursuline Nuns, represented by Sister Monica Namos, purchased a "lot of ground in Bourbon Street, having 60 foot front on Bourbon Street, by 120 feet in depth. Bounded by the lands of Agatha Lenelle, free quadroon, and Ramon Eacott." Then a record dated April 20, 1799, reveals "a house, of 20 foot front, divided into one hall, two apartments, two cabinets, and one gallery, constructed on a lot of 20 feet front on Bourbon Street by a depth of 160 feet." In 1836, Joseph Lombard, Sr., purchased the property for $4,000. It is generally conceded that Lombard renovated whatever house existed at the time into something that resembles the one standing today — a typical Vieux Carré two-story town house, simple and well proportioned, with Greek Revival detailing and an iron grillwork balcony spanning the upper story.

Opposite: *Entrance hall.* **Above:** *Front upstairs balcony.* **Right:** *Topiary.* **Below:** *Living room mantel with African sculptures.*

Grilled Veal Chop with Smoked Tomato Sauce

Sweet and simple. Have your butcher "French" the chops.

6 10-ounce veal chops, including bone
2 tablespoons unsalted butter, melted
Salt and black pepper to taste
Smoked Tomato Sauce (recipe follows)

Preheat the grill or oven broiler. Brush all sides of the chops with butter and season with salt and pepper. Grill for 8 to 10 minutes, turning once. Serve with Smoked Tomato Sauce.

Serves 6

Smoked Tomato Sauce

6 to 7 medium vine-ripened tomatoes, smoked
   (recipe follows)
1½ teaspoons minced fresh thyme
1½ medium bay leaves
¼ teaspoon Creole Seasoning (page 109)
1 tablespoon plus ¾ teaspoon paprika
1 teaspoon minced garlic
Pinch of cayenne pepper or a good dash of Tabasco
2 tablespoons rich chicken stock
2 tablespoons rice wine vinegar
2 tablespoons heavy cream
½ to ¾ cup (1 to 1½ sticks) unsalted butter,
   chilled and cut into bits

Place a fine strainer over a bowl. Holding the tomatoes over it, slip the skins off and squeeze the seeds out. Place skinned and seeded tomato pulp, and the tomato liquid that has been strained of seeds, in a medium saucepan along with the herbs and seasonings. Simmer over medium-low heat for 5 or 6 minutes to reduce and thicken slightly.

Remove from the heat, discard the bay leaves, and puree the mixture. Return it to the saucepan and stir in the stock and vinegar. Simmer another 6 to 8 minutes to thicken. Off the heat, whisk in the cream and then the bits of butter until well emulsified. Serve immediately.

Makes about 2 cups

Smoked Tomatoes

To smoke tomatoes without a regular smoker, use a charcoal grill with a cover and make a fire of charcoal.

Cut the core out of your tomatoes and use the point of a knife to score an X in the other end, just cutting through the skin. When the coals have burned down and are white with ash, cover with moistened wood chips. Place tomatoes, cored end up, on a rack and cover grill with its lid. Crack vents to about ¼ inch. Smoke tomatoes, checking every few minutes to make sure fire is smoking properly and not flaring up, for about 35 to 45 minutes.

Tomatoes are ready when skins begin to wrinkle, and they begin to collapse but are still whole and have not turned mushy. Add more wood chips if necessary. Allow to cool. Store in the refrigerator until ready to use.

Roasted Potatoes

Crunchy on the outside and smooth within.

1 tablespoon vegetable oil
1 tablespoon unsalted butter
12 whole small white potatoes, peeled
Salt to taste

Preheat oven to 400 degrees.

In an ovenproof skillet large enough to hold all the potatoes in a single layer, heat oil and butter over high heat. Add potatoes and roll them around to coat. Place pan in the oven and roast about 15 minutes, until done. Shake the pan frequently to make sure the potatoes brown evenly. Salt to taste.

Serves 6

Above: *Grilled Veal Chop with Smoked Tomato Sauce, Roasted Potatoes, and Sautéed Kohlrabi.* **Below:** *Period side chair.*

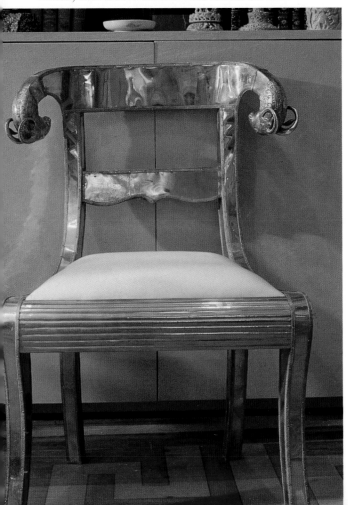

Sautéed Kohlrabi

Kohlrabi has a distinctive flavor that I especially like. When you see it in your market give it a try prepared in this uncomplicated way.

2 cups kohlrabi, peeled and cut into ½-inch dice
1 tablespoon unsalted butter
Salt to taste
¼ teaspoon white pepper
1 tablespoon minced parsley

Cover kohlrabi with salted water and bring quickly to a boil. Turn the heat to medium and cook until tender, about 8 minutes. Drain and keep warm, covered with a damp tea towel. To serve, melt butter in a medium skillet and sauté kohlrabi, tossing, until heated. Sprinkle with salt and pepper and toss with the parsley.

Serves 6

Mixed Greens with Champagne Vinaigrette

Here there is Boston lettuce, frisée, and oak leaf lettuce with the extra fillip of sliced, seeded cucumber, but you can use any combination of greens in your market.

3 tablespoons Champagne vinegar
½ cup olive oil
½ teaspoon salt
Pinch of black pepper
2 teaspoons minced red onion
5 cups mixed greens
1 small cucumber, peeled, seeded, and cut into medium-
 thick half rings

Whisk together the vinegar, oil, salt, and pepper. Stir in the onion.
 Toss greens and cucumber together, then spoon enough vinaigrette over all to coat greens when they are tossed.

Serves 6

Chocolate Mousse Cake

Yet another version of almost everyone's favorite.

Cake

1 cup (2 sticks) unsalted butter, softened
1 cup sugar
1 teaspoon vanilla extract
2 eggs
1 cup cake flour
1 cup cocoa powder
1 teaspoon baking powder
½ teaspoon baking soda
½ cup sour cream

Mousse

¾ pound semisweet chocolate, melted and cooled
  slightly
3 egg yolks, lightly beaten
¼ cup (½ stick) unsalted butter, melted
1 cup heavy cream
1 tablespoon sugar

Frosting

¾ pound semisweet chocolate, chopped coarsely
¼ cup (½ stick) unsalted butter, softened
½ cup milk, at room temperature
½ cup heavy cream, at room temperature

Assembly

2 tablespoons Madeira
Seedless raspberry jam

Preheat oven to 350 degrees. Butter and flour a
9 x 3-inch cake pan.

Make the cake: With a hand mixer, cream together
the butter and sugar until light and fluffy. Beat in
vanilla, then the eggs, one at a time. Sift flour, cocoa,
baking powder, and soda. Add the flour mixture,
alternately with the sour cream, to the butter
mixture, beginning and ending with flour. Do not
overmix.

Scrape the batter into the prepared pan and bake
until tester comes out clean, about 40 minutes.
Cool, loosen edges, and turn cake out. Slice into 3
layers and set aside.

Make the mousse: Mix together the chocolate and egg
yolks. Stir in melted butter and set aside. Whip
together the cream and sugar until it stands in soft

peaks. Fold about one-quarter of the cream into the
chocolate mixture to lighten it and then fold in the
balance with a light touch. Set aside.

Make the frosting: Place the chocolate in the top of a
double boiler and melt, stirring. Off the heat, stir in
butter, milk, and cream. Mix well and set aside at
room temperature.

Assemble: Put first layer on a cake plate and sprinkle
with half the Madeira. Spread with a very thin layer
of jam and then with one-third of the mousse. Put
the second layer on, holding it in place with
toothpicks if necessary, and repeat as with the first
layer. Top with the third layer. Spread remaining
mousse generously over the top and thinly on the
sides. Chill for at least an hour. Spread frosting over
all. Chill again for at least 30 minutes before serving.

Cut with a knife that has been dipped in hot water
and wiped dry.

Serves 12 or more

Below: *Garden fountain with potted impatiens.*
Opposite: *Chocolate Mousse Cake*

PASTA WITH A BAYOU TWIST
Pitot House

Crawfish Fettuccine

Endive, Radicchio, Apple, and Pepper with Blue Cheese Vinaigrette

Mixed Berry Shortcake

Sonoma-Cutrer 1988 Chardonnay

New Orleans has its ubiquitous pizza places, but for almost as long as I can remember, the only Italian food people here really seemed to like was spaghetti and meatballs. I'm not knocking it; as a matter of fact, I still *think* I have a weakness for it — but frankly, this is probably based more on remembered good times than the actual food. ∾ As I've said elsewhere in this book, the moment seems just about right for an infusion of Northern Italian style into New Orleans cooking. And since crawfish *étouffée* is served on rice, what about spicy crawfish on pasta? Now this is a pretty rich combination so I don't think you'd want anything with it except a bit of Italian bread and maybe butter. A little green salad is welcome before the delightful mixed berry shortcake. I know — you think you couldn't possibly. Trust me.

Above: *Crawfish Fettuccine.* **Opposite:** *Storm shutters.*

Crawfish Fettuccine

*Luckily, cooked and peeled crawfish tails are
sold frozen in many specialty markets today. If you
can't find them nearby you can order them from
Craig Borges at New Orleans Fish House,
1020 Erate Street, New Orleans, LA 70130
(telephone 504-524-8027).*

½ cup (1 stick) plus 2 tablespoons cold unsalted butter,
   cut into 5 or 6 pieces
½ cup diced green pepper
½ cup diced red pepper
1 cup diced onion
1½ pounds cooked and peeled crawfish tails
½ teaspoon Creole Seasoning (page 109)
¼ teaspoon crushed red pepper flakes
½ teaspoon salt
1 cup peeled, seeded, and diced tomato
6 tablespoons thinly sliced green onion
12 ounces dry fettuccine
6 whole cooked crawfish for garnish (optional)

Put up a large pot of water to boil while you prepare
the sauce. In a large skillet, melt 2 tablespoons of
the butter and sauté the peppers and onion over high
heat, stirring, for 2 or 3 minutes, until well wilted.
Add crawfish tails, Creole Seasoning, pepper flakes,
and salt. Turn down heat and cook for 2 to 3
minutes. Add the tomato and green onion and
continue to cook. Stir in the bits of butter one by
one. When all is incorporated, turn off heat. Cook
fettuccine according to package directions.

   Place fettuccine on individual plates. Surround and
top with the sauce. Garnish with a whole crawfish if
you like.

Serves 6

**Note: There is a little trick restaurants use to make serving
individual portions of pasta easier. They cook whatever
amount required al dente, plunge it into cold water, drain it,
and then toss the pasta with about 1 tablespoon of vegetable
oil to keep it limber and from sticking together. Just before
serving the pasta, they place it in a colander and lower it
back into hot water just long enough to heat it through,
about 5 to 10 seconds.**

Endive, Radicchio, Apple, and Pepper with Blue Cheese Vinaigrette

This is a delicious combination.

2 heads Belgian endive, leaves separated
1 small head radicchio, leaves separated
1 medium tart apple, peeled, cored, and diced
½ medium yellow bell pepper, seeded and cut into
   thin julienne
3 tablespoons vegetable oil
1 tablespoon rice wine vinegar
¼ teaspoon black pepper
4 ounces crumbled Roquefort cheese

Toss endive, radicchio, apple, and yellow pepper
together in a large salad bowl.
   Make the vinaigrette by whisking together all the
other ingredients except cheese. Stir in cheese.
   Toss salad again with vinaigrette.

Serves 6

Above: *Flowers on the mantel.*

Above: *Upstairs gallery.* **Below:** *Endive, Radicchio, Apple, and Pepper with Blue Cheese Vinaigrette.*
Overleaf: *Drawing room sofa at left; summer rockers at right.*

ABOUT THE HOUSE

Although the building is known as the Pitot House, James Pitot — second mayor of New Orleans — was not its builder or its first owner. What's more, the house isn't even where it was built (sometime around 1795); it was moved lock, stock, and barrel to its present site in 1964.

Legend has it that Bartholome Bosque — who turns up as a player in the history of the Sauvinet-Baus House (page 72) — started the house. It's not really known who designed it or if it was even finished before Bosque sold it in 1800. Five years later it was purchased by Marie Tronquet-Rillieux, great-grandmother of the painter Edgar Degas. It's generally believed that Mme. Rillieux was responsible for the extensive changes to the building, perhaps even adding the gallery along its right side. When she finished, though, the house probably looked pretty much like it does today.

For whatever reason, no sooner was the house finished than it was sold to the Pitot family, who gave it their name — James Pitot being the most illustrious resident. The property had been offered for sale repeatedly until it was acquired by the present owners and given landmark status and protection.

Opposite: *Pitot House.* **Above:** *Mixed Berry Shortcake.*

Mixed Berry Shortcake

Use any combination of berries you like for this.

2 cups all-purpose flour
2 tablespoons sugar, plus additional for berries
¼ teaspoon salt
4 teaspoons baking powder
2 eggs, lightly beaten
4 tablespoons (½ stick) unsalted butter, chilled and
   cut into small pieces
⅓ to ½ cup heavy cream, plus 1½ cups for whipping
2 pints mixed berries

Preheat oven to 400 degrees.
   Mix dry ingredients together in a large bowl. Stir

in eggs, mixing. Cut butter in with a pastry blender
or 2 knives. Mix in enough cream to make a dry
dough. Roll out ½ inch thick on a floured surface
and cut into 8 or 9 biscuits. Place on an ungreased
baking sheet and bake until golden, about 12
minutes.
   Whip the cream and refrigerate; sweeten the
berries to taste and refrigerate.
   To serve, split the biscuits. Place the bottom half
on a dessert plate and cover with berries and some
of their juice. Replace top and add more berries and
a dollop of whipped cream sweetened with a
teaspoon or two of sugar.

Serves 8

A SOFT-SHELL CRAB SUPPER

Rey-Ochsner House

Baked Jalapeño
Oysters on the Half Shell

Soft-Shell Crabs
with Lemon Butter Sauce

Mixed Wild and Long-Grain Rice

Buttermilk Pie

De Loach O.F.S. 1989 Chardonnay

In the last few years, soft-shell crawfish have become popular in this part of the world, but as tempting as they are, they still can't compare to soft-shell crabs in my view. So soft-shell crabs are what we have for this menu. ∾ There are a number of methods for cooking soft-shells that produce excellent results, such as a simple sauté in butter or a fry of cornmeal-coated crabs. This time around the crabs are stuffed with more crabmeat, lightly coated with spicy flour, and deep-fried to a golden finish. They are served with a lemon butter sauce and accompanied by a combination of wild and long-grain rice that I like so much I have it for lunch with some sliced tomatoes — you might want to give it a try that way. ∾ To begin the meal are oysters topped with jalapeño sauce and baked on the half shell. Baked oysters are particularly pleasing, and since some folks are uneasy about eating oysters raw, baking may be the best of all options. ∾ To end the meal is a zesty buttermilk pie, the flavor of which is a nice finish for a seafood menu.

Opposite: *Baked Jalapeño Oysters on the Half Shell.*

Baked Jalapeño Oysters on the Half Shell

A delicious new take on traditional baked oysters.

4 ounces slab bacon, cut into small dice

½ cup minced red onion

¼ cup seeded and minced jalapeño pepper

½ cup each diced red and green bell pepper

7 tablespoons unsalted butter

6 tablespoons flour

2 cups milk

1 cup heavy cream

½ teaspoon salt

½ teaspoon white pepper

1¼ cups peeled, seeded, and chopped tomato

¼ cup grated Romano cheese

¼ teaspoon Louisiana Hot Sauce

⅓ cup dry bread crumbs

1 pound fresh spinach, stemmed and torn into
  large pieces

18 fresh shucked oysters, shells reserved

Rock salt for baking

In a medium skillet, cook the bacon over medium heat until crisp. Pour out all but 2 tablespoons of the fat. Add the onion, jalapeño, and bell peppers. Cook over medium heat until wilted, about 5 minutes. Set aside.

Melt 6 tablespoons of the butter in a medium saucepan over low heat; stir in the flour and turn heat up to medium. Whisk in milk and cream and continue to cook, whisking, for 8 minutes. Stir in vegetables and continue to cook until thickened, another 6 to 8 minutes. Add salt, pepper, and chopped tomato and cook, stirring, another 2 minutes. Off the heat, stir in half the cheese and the hot sauce. Taste for seasoning and add more salt, pepper, or hot sauce. Mix the remaining cheese with the bread crumbs. Set aside.

Preheat oven to 450 degrees.

Rinse spinach and shake off water. Melt remaining tablespoon of butter in a large skillet and add spinach. Cover, shaking pan, until wilted slightly.

Scrub 18 of the reserved shells. To bake, cover bottom of a baking sheet with rock salt and arrange shells on it. Divide spinach among the shells and top each with an oyster. Sprinkle oysters with half the cheese-crumb mixture. Top each with a generous

tablespoon of the sauce and sprinkle with the balance of the cheese-crumb mixture. Bake for 8 to 10 minutes. Turn on broiler and cook for about another minute to brown tops lightly.

Serves 6 to 8

Soft-Shell Crabs with Lemon Butter Sauce

These are easy to make, and they look very impressive.

6 soft-shell crabs, washed and trimmed

Stuffing
4 ounces claw crabmeat, picked over
1 egg
¾ cup diced green pepper
2 tablespoons mayonnaise
½ cup dry bread crumbs
1 teaspoon Creole Seasoning (page 109)

Coating
½ cup corn flour
1 cup all-purpose flour
½ cup cornstarch
½ teaspoon black pepper
½ teaspoon salt
1 teaspoon Creole mustard (see Note, page 87)
½ teaspoon garlic powder
1 teaspoon paprika
2 eggs
1½ cups milk

Vegetable oil for deep-frying
Lemon Butter Sauce (recipe follows)

Trim the crabs by removing eyes, tail, and gills under the top shell, leaving a small cavity.
  Make the stuffing: Mix together all the ingredients for the stuffing and stuff the crabs.
  Make the coating and fry: Mix all dry ingredients together in a bowl; beat together the eggs and milk in a separate bowl. Dust stuffed crabs carefully in flour mixture; dip them in the egg wash and coat once more in the flour mixture.

Heat oil in a deep fryer to 375 degrees. Fry crabs until golden, about 4 minutes. Serve with Lemon Butter Sauce.

Serves 6

Lemon Butter Sauce
2 tablespoons cream
¾ cup (1½ sticks) unsalted butter, chilled and cut into bits
2 tablespoons fresh lemon juice
Salt and black pepper to taste

In a small heavy saucepan, heat cream over low flame until boiling; whisk in half the butter. Remove from heat and whisk in the balance of the butter, and lemon juice and seasonings. Serve warm.

Opposite: *Detail of carved window frame.* **Below:** *Entrance hall.*

ABOUT THE HOUSE

The history of this house is tough to track. Square 105, as it was designated, appeared on something called the de la Tour Map as being granted to M. Le Breton, M. Trudot, and M. Monbrun of St. Laurent in 1722. After that tantalizing mention, the property turns up sporadically in the record books as unassigned until 1847, when Mme. Marie Celeste St. Amand, divorced wife of Arthur Fortier, sold whatever there was to Claude François Rey. There is nothing to indicate how Madame acquired the title or even if there was a building on the land. However, the style of the house indicates that it was built around 1830, so the sale to M. Rey probably did include a house. But there is no record of who built the house, or when, and apparently there were no scandals worth writing or litigating over.

When you look at the place — a well-proportioned Greek Revival house with three patios marching back — you do have to wonder how something so large and impressive could have come into being and left so little behind to say for itself.

Here are the details we know: The black and white tiles on the floor downstairs are Mexican, and the interior shutters on some of the downstairs windows came from an upriver plantation. This is gleaned from a few dusty unattributed clippings. Someone obviously knew at one time but didn't think it important enough to go into detail.

What you see is what you get — which is fine, but you can't help but wish for a bit more.

Opposite: *Slave quarters.* **Above:** *Soft-Shell Crabs with Lemon Butter Sauce and Mixed Wild and Long-Grain Rice.*

Mixed Wild and Long-Grain Rice

This could also become the basis of a stuffing for chicken or turkey.

1½ cups long-grain rice

½ cup wild rice

2 tablespoons unsalted butter

4 ounces andouille sausage, removed from casing
    and chopped

¼ cup *each* minced red bell pepper, green bell pepper,
    red onion, zucchini, and yellow squash

¼ teaspoon salt

¼ teaspoon black pepper

⅔ cup chicken stock

Preheat oven to 250 degrees.

Cover long-grain rice with 3½ cups well-salted
water. Bring to a boil over high heat. Turn the heat
down to a slow boil and cook until tender, 12 to 15
minutes. Drain, rinse, and set aside.

Cover wild rice with 1½ cups well-salted water.
Bring to a boil over high heat. Turn the heat down
to a slow boil and cook until tender, 12 to 15
minutes. Drain, rinse, and combine with white rice.
Set aside.

Melt butter in a large skillet and add sausage.
Cook over medium heat, stirring, until browned,
about 3 minutes. Add vegetables and continue to
cook, tossing lightly, until softened, about 3
minutes.

Reheat rices by putting them in a strainer and
immersing in boiling water, off the heat, for 1
minute. Drain. Mix the rices with the sausage and
vegetables. Season with salt and pepper. Put into a
greased ovenproof casserole and add the stock.
Cover and heat for 20 minutes.

Serves 6 to 8

Above: *Buttermilk Pie.* **Below:** *Sofa in the front living room.* **Opposite:** *Lush patio plants.*

Buttermilk Pie

*Top this pie with a dab of whipped cream or
berry puree — or both!*

Pastry

1 cup all-purpose flour
1 teaspoon salt
½ cup (1 stick) unsalted butter, chilled and cut into bits
1 egg yolk, lightly beaten
¼ cup cold water

Filling

4 egg yolks
1 cup sugar
½ cup all-purpose flour
3 tablespoons unsalted butter, melted
½ teaspoon baking soda
2 cups buttermilk
2 tablespoons fresh lemon juice
1 teaspoon vanilla extract

Make the pastry: Put flour and salt into the bowl of a
food processor and pulse once or twice to mix.
Add butter and process just long enough for mixture
to become mealy. Mix the egg yolk with the water
and pour in, pulsing just until the mixture starts to
cling together. Gather into a ball and flatten between
2 sheets of waxed paper. Refrigerate for an hour or
two.

Preheat oven to 350 degrees.

Roll pastry out on a floured surface and line a
9-inch pie pan with it. Place a parchment circle over
dough and weight down with pie weights or dry
beans. Bake for about 10 minutes, until set. Remove
parchment and beans. Continue baking until crust
is golden, about 30 minutes more. Place on a rack
to cool.

Preheat oven to 425 degrees.

Make the filling: Beat yolks until light and lemony in
color. Combine sugar and flour and gradually beat
into eggs. Mix in butter. Dissolve the baking soda in
the buttermilk and add to the egg mixture. Stir in
lemon juice and vanilla. Pour into baked pie shell
and bake 8 minutes. Turn heat down to 350 degrees
and bake until a knife inserted into the center comes
out clean, about 40 minutes. Cool.

Serves 8

E A R L Y   D I N N E R

Sauvinet-Baus House

Broiled Scallops with Beggars' Purses

Nasturtium Salad

Apple Cobbler

Cinnamon Ice Cream

Mondavi "Reserve" Sauvignon Blanc, Napa 1989

Although everyone knows how very popular fish and seafood are here, scallops — that Eastern favorite — have always been rather neglected. Maybe there was just too much competition from the local stuff. So I suggested we use these tender little morsels for an entree, and I was amused when we finally settled on how they were to be served — with beggars' purses filled with crabmeat. It was a mouth-watering combination, further proof of that New Orleans saw: If one kind of seafood is good, two are terrific. ❧ Should you be in the mood for an appetizer and small asparagus are in season, try little bundles of them wrapped with a cummerbund of prosciutto and broiled. ❧ After the scallops there was a colorful salad and, finally, one of those desserts this place is famous for, a cobbler, made with apples. That would have been sufficient, but we thought, what about a little cinnamon ice cream to go along with it? Might as well go all the way. ❧ An elegant small meal for a house that has reclaimed its beauty and peace of mind.

Left: *Oak leaf hydrangea.* **Opposite:** *Broiled Scallops with Beggars' Purses.*

Above: *Nasturtium Salad.* **Below:** *French dining room chairs.*

Broiled Scallops with Beggars' Purses

If you can only find large sea scallops, cut them in half.

1½ pounds small sea scallops, washed and trimmed
2 tablespoons olive oil
5 tablespoons vegetable oil
½ cup snipped chervil
Black pepper to taste
½ teaspoon salt
8 ounces crabmeat, picked over
3 tablespoons minced red bell pepper
1½ tablespoons minced chervil, plus extra for garnish
3 tablespoons mayonnaise
2 teaspoons fresh lemon juice
Salt to taste
½ teaspoon white pepper
12 squares phyllo dough, about 6 by 6 inches each
½ cup (1 stick) unsalted butter, melted
6 long strips of chives
Butter Sauce (recipe follows)
Lemon wedges for garnish (optional)

Place scallops in a bowl with oils and the ½ cup chervil. Sprinkle with the black pepper and ½ teaspoon salt. Mix with your hands or 2 forks to coat thoroughly and allow to marinate at room temperature for 1 hour.

Meanwhile, mix together the crabmeat, red bell pepper, the 1½ tablespoons minced chervil, mayonnaise, lemon juice, salt, and white pepper.

Brush one phyllo square lightly with the melted butter (keep remainder covered with a damp cloth). Place a second square on top at a 45-degree angle (this will look like an 8-pointed star) and brush lightly with butter. Put a heaping tablespoon of the crab mixture in the center. Pull up the dough and gather it together to enclose the filling. Squeeze it slightly to make a little neck, leaving the points sticking up. Soak chives in hot water for about 30 seconds to make them pliable and knot the neck closed with one. Place on a metal pie tin. Repeat the process to make 5 more purses (these may be made up to 2 hours in advance).

Preheat oven to 375 degrees. Bake beggars' purses until heated through and just beginning to turn golden, about 10 to 12 minutes.

Meanwhile, place marinated scallops in a single layer on a low-sided broiler pan (do not crowd). As soon as the purses come out of the oven, turn on broiler and cook scallops for 2 to 3 minutes, just to heat through. Do not let brown.

To serve, place a purse in the middle of a plate and surround with scallops. Top scallops with a bit of Butter Sauce and garnish with a lemon wedge.

Serves 6

Butter Sauce

¼ cup cream
⅓ cup unsalted butter, cut into bits
¼ teaspoon salt
Pinch of white pepper
2 to 3 tablespoons fresh lemon juice

Heat cream in a small saucepan over a low flame and whisk in butter. Stir in salt, pepper, and lemon juice. Keep warm, but not over a direct flame.

Nasturtium Salad

Now here is a very refreshing combination. The nasturtium adds a peppery bite.

1 small head radicchio, in bite-size pieces
1 small head red leaf lettuce, in bite-size pieces
1 bunch mâche, roots cut off
1½ cup nasturtium leaves and flowers
2 tablespoons red wine vinegar
1 teaspoon minced garlic
1½ teaspoons minced onion
½ teaspoon Dijon-style mustard
½ teaspoon salt
Pinch of black pepper
½ teaspoon minced fresh thyme
1 teaspoon minced parsley
6 tablespoons olive oil

Whisk together the vinegar, garlic, onion, and seasonings. Slowly drizzle in the olive oil, whisking until combined. Adjust seasoning if necessary. If using in the next few hours do not refrigerate.

To serve, toss greens with enough vinaigrette to coat well.

Serves 6

Above left: *Pruned pittosparum.* **Above:** *Flower-filled patio.*

ABOUT THE HOUSE

Here are some highlights from the convoluted history of the Sauvinet-Baus House. Sometime in 1803, a Frenchman named Bartholome Bosque sold a parcel of land to the Sauvinets, newly arrived from France. One assumes the Sauvinets built during the next year or so, which means what remains of the original house dates from about 1804. Evidence suggests this first structure was erected in what is now the front garden, probably right at the street, with slave quarters in the rear separated by a courtyard. (However, we *do* know that Sauvinet was the pirate Jean Lafitte's lawyer — for what good that does us.)

The front house burned to the ground sometime after 1822. Over the ensuing twenty or so years a modest cottage was added to the side of the remaining slave quarters and several other smaller structures were sprinkled around. All of these together comprise the house you see today.

Everything pretty much goes blank until 1884,

by which time the property had passed into the possession of the Sauvinets' daughter Camille. Here the plot thickens and litigation followed, almost right up to the middle of this century. Camille signed a bill of sale believing it was something else; this had to be unraveled. Then she signed it over to one son as collateral for a loan. The other son relinquished his claim on the property so it could go to his "generous" brother but decades later he decided he had been duped and tried to have this gesture voided. That failed. Anyway, the "generous" son went on to marry and have five daughters, all of whom wound up in the funny farm. Are you still with me? But before it was all over, the property had been pulled back and forth, disclosures had been made and knocked down, and the lawyers had had a merry old time.

Today, though, all is serene and blooming, and this lovely place is at peace.

Apple Cobbler

*You can make this in individual servings as
we did for the photograph, but frankly at home I don't
think it's worth the trouble. I always just make
it in a single dish.*

1 cup (2 sticks) plus 2 tablespoons unsalted
   butter, chilled

2 egg yolks

1 teaspoon salt

3 cups flour

2 to 3 tablespoons ice water

6 cups thin-sliced peeled and cored tart apples

1 tablespoon lemon juice

1 teaspoon grated lemon zest

1 cup sugar

1 teaspoon cinnamon

Preheat oven to 400 degrees.

   Cut 1 cup of the butter into small pieces and place
in the bowl of a food processor with the yolks.
Process until smooth. Sprinkle salt over all and add
flour; pulse to mix coarsely. Sprinkle water over all
and pulse until mixture just begins to cling together.
Form into a ball, wrap in plastic wrap, and
refrigerate. Toss apples with the lemon juice, zest,
sugar, and cinnamon. Set aside.

   Unwrap dough and roll out into a 15-inch circle
between 2 sheets of waxed paper. Line an 8-cup
soufflé dish with the dough, allowing the excess to
drape over the edges. If dough breaks, patch it.
Dump in apple mixture and dot with the remaining
2 tablespoons of butter. Flop dough on top of the
apples, using any pieces that may have broken off.

   Bake until apples are soft, about 1 hour.

   Serve with Cinnamon Ice Cream or whipped
cream.

Serves 8

Right: *Apple Cobbler
with Cinnamon Ice
Cream.*

Cinnamon Ice Cream

This is perfect with apple pie or cobbler.

2 cups heavy cream

2 cups half-and-half

¾ cup sugar

3 whole eggs

3 egg yolks

¼ cup honey

2 tablespoons cinnamon

2 tablespoons hot water

Combine cream, half-and-half, and ½ cup of the
sugar in a saucepan and scald over medium heat,
stirring.

   Slightly beat eggs, yolks, and remaining sugar in a
stainless steel bowl. Add a cup of the scalded cream
mixture to the eggs, whisking lightly. Add egg
mixture to the remainder of the scalded mixture.
Whisk. Combine honey, cinnamon, and hot water
and whisk this in. Strain, press a piece of plastic
wrap onto the surface, and allow to cool. Chill in
the refrigerator. Pour into an ice cream maker and
freeze according to manufacturer's instructions.

Makes 1 generous quart

Crab Corn Bisque.

NEW ORLEANS SOUPS

New Orleanians like their soups hearty, and so do I. These either have to be eaten in small portions or should be the main course. Main course is what I prefer. See for yourself.

Crab Corn Bisque

Since you must go to the bother of making a stock base, this recipe is for a large quantity. But that's fine, because this soup freezes well.

Stock
2 tablespoons unsalted butter
1 pound onions, peeled and chopped coarse
2 large celery ribs, chopped coarse
8 large garlic cloves, peeled
2 ½ pounds smashed blue crab shells (the yield from 5 to 6 pounds fresh whole crabs)
1 cup dry white wine
½ gallon water
1 tablespoon minced fresh thyme
½ cup whole peppercorns
3 large bay leaves

Roux
½ cup unsalted clarified butter
½ cup all-purpose flour

Bisque
4 tablespoons unsalted butter
Kernels from 3 ears of corn, or 10 ounces frozen, thawed
1 bunch green onions, julienned, with a lot of green
1 pound crabmeat, picked over
⅓ cup brandy
3 tablespoons Louisiana Hot Sauce
Salt and black pepper to taste

Make the stock: Melt butter in a 10-quart stock pot over high heat. Sauté onions, celery, garlic, and crab shells for about 5 minutes, until the vegetables are translucent. Add wine, water, and seasonings. Bring back to a boil, then reduce heat to a simmer. Cook for 30 minutes, skimming occasionally. Strain, discarding solids. Reserve stock.

Make the roux: Melt butter in a large skillet over medium heat. Add flour a few tablespoons at a time, whisking all the while. Continue to cook and whisk until mixture turns dark golden. Set aside.

Complete the bisque: Melt butter in a 10-quart stock pot over medium heat. Add the corn and onions and sauté until corn is tender, about 2 minutes. Add crabmeat and stir; add brandy and stir. Cook another couple of minutes. Add the reserved stock and bring to a simmer. Stir in roux, whisking to

avoid lumps. Simmer for another 30 minutes. Off the heat, stir in the hot sauce, and salt and pepper to taste.

Serves 12

Crawfish Bisque

This is another soup that freezes well.

Stock

5 pounds live crawfish
1 large head of garlic, cloves peeled and chopped coarse
3 large celery ribs, chopped coarse
1 pound onions, peeled and chopped coarse
3 large bay leaves, crumbled
¼ cup black peppercorns
1½ gallons of water

Roux

2 medium green bell peppers, finely chopped
¾ pound celery ribs, finely chopped
2 pounds onions, finely chopped
16 medium garlic cloves, about 1½ heads, peeled and minced
2½ cups peanut oil
3 cups flour
2 tablespoons Creole Seasoning (page 109)
2 tablespoons Worcestershire sauce
1 cup peeled, seeded, and chopped tomato

Stuffed Crawfish Heads (recipe follows)

Make the stock: Plunge crawfish into boiling water. Cook for 1½ minutes. Drain and reserve 3 dozen heads. Peel enough tails, reserving shells, to get 1 pound of meat. Set aside.

Put shells and the remaining whole boiled crawfish in a large stock pot with the garlic, celery, onions, bay leaves, and peppercorns. Sauté, mashing and chopping with a large spoon, over high heat for about 1 to 2 minutes. Add the water, bring to a boil, and simmer for 30 minutes. Strain and keep warm.

Make the roux: Toss all the chopped vegetables together in a large bowl. Heat oil in a large heavy pot to the smoking point. Add flour gradually, about ½ cup at a time, stirring constantly with a wooden spoon. Turn heat down to medium and

Crawfish Bisque.

continue to cook, stirring, until roux is a dark color. Dump in the reserved vegetables, stir and remove from heat. Stir in warm stock. Return to stove and continue to simmer over medium heat until thickened, about 4 minutes. Stir in seasonings and the chopped tomato.

Serve garnished with Stuffed Crawfish Heads.

Serves 12

Stuffed Crawfish Heads

½ cup (1 stick) unsalted butter
2 tablespoons minced garlic
1 medium celery rib, diced
½ medium onion, diced
½ medium green bell pepper, diced
1 pound crawfish tails (reserved from bisque), chopped coarse
1 tablespoon Creole Seasoning (page 109)
½ teaspoon salt
½ teaspoon cayenne pepper
1½ cups dry bread crumbs
½ egg white
3 dozen crawfish heads (reserved from bisque)

Preheat oven to 350 degrees.

Heat butter in a large heavy skillet over medium heat and stir in vegetables. Sauté until translucent, about 4 minutes. Stir in crawfish tails, seasonings, and 1 cup of the bread crumbs. Remove from heat and mix lightly. Mix in egg white. Stuff heads with mixture and roll in the remaining bread crumbs. Place on a baking sheet and bake for 4 to 5 minutes, until heated through and browned.

Cream of Roasted Eggplant Soup.

Cream of Roasted Eggplant Soup

*The hearty chicken stock used in this soup may
be made in advance.*

Stock

1 3-pound chicken
⅓ cup tomato paste
3 medium celery ribs, chopped coarse
1 pound onions, peeled and chopped coarse
2 large carrots, unpeeled and chopped coarse
2 cups dry red wine
1 bay leaf
4 sprigs parsley
1 teaspoon dried thyme
¼ cup black peppercorns
1½ gallons water

To finish

1 large eggplant, peeled
1 large onion, peeled
1 large head garlic, with top ¼ inch cut off
2 tablespoons olive oil
3 quarts reduced chicken stock
½ cup vegetable oil
½ cup flour
1 cup heavy cream
½ teaspoon curry powder
1 tablespoon Louisiana Hot Sauce
Salt and white pepper to taste
⅓ cup minced green onion, mostly green

Make the stock: Preheat oven to 400 degrees.

Bone the chicken, reserving the meat for another
use. Chop the carcass and wings and rub the pieces
with tomato paste. Put them in a roasting pan with
the celery, onions, and carrots. Roast for 40 minutes,
turning occasionally.

Pour all fat from pan and put pan over a
medium flame. Deglaze with the red wine. Pour
all into a 10-quart stock pot and add bay leaf,
parsley, thyme, peppercorns, and water. Bring to a
boil, then turn the heat down to a simmer. Cook
for 1½ hours, skimming occasionally. Strain
through a fine sieve. Set aside.

Finish the soup: Reduce the reserved stock by half
over high heat. Preheat oven to 350 degrees.

Rub the whole eggplant, onion, and garlic with
the olive oil and place on a greased baking sheet.
(The garlic should be cut side up.) Bake for 30
minutes until eggplant is tender. Remove and
puree. Continue to roast garlic and onion until
each is tender, about another 15 to 20 minutes
for the garlic and another 30 minutes for the
onion. Squeeze out garlic and puree with the
onion. Mix both purees together in a large stock
pot and stir in reduced stock. Bring to a simmer.

Meanwhile, combine oil and flour in a heavy
skillet and cook over high heat, constantly moving
around and scraping the bottom of the skillet
with a spatula. When it's golden and smelling
nutty, whisk into the simmering stock. Be careful
here as it will boil up.

Continue to cook for another 5 minutes. Stir in
heavy cream, curry powder, hot sauce, salt, and
pepper and remove from the heat. Serve sprinkled
with minced green onion.

If you would like to freeze this, omit the cream.
Add it when you reheat the soup.

Serves 12

Oysters Rockefeller Soup.

Gumbo Ya Ya

The classic.

¼ cup vegetable oil
3 3-pound chickens, chopped into large pieces
2 tablespoons Creole Seasoning (page 109)
2¼ cups peanut oil
3 cups flour
2 pounds onions, peeled and cut into medium dice
1 pound celery ribs, cut into medium dice
3 tablespoons minced garlic
5 quarts boiling water
3 tablespoons salt
1 tablespoon cayenne pepper
1 pound andouille sausage, cut into ¼-inch rings
1 tablespoon gumbo filé

Heat vegetable oil in a large saucepan. Rub chicken pieces with the Creole Seasoning. Add to the oil and brown, turning, several minutes. Set aside off the heat.

In a heavy skillet, combine the peanut oil and flour. Make a dark roux (page 79). When about as dark as a roasted pecan, scrape the roux immediately into a 10-gallon stock pot. Stir in vegetables and mix. Carefully pour in the water. Stir to dissolve roux. Add the seasonings and the chicken along with any juices it has given up. Simmer over low heat for 45 minutes. Along the way, skim off and discard any oil that may rise to the top. Add sausage and simmer another 12 minutes. Whisk in the filé.

Serve with hot sauce on the side.

Serves 12 or more

Oysters Rockefeller Soup

This soup can't be frozen but the recipe is easily halved.

4 tablespoons unsalted butter
2 pounds onions, peeled and diced
1½ pounds celery, diced
¾ cup Pernod
8 cups oyster water or bottled clam juice (or a combination of the two)
4 teaspoons salt
1 teaspoon white pepper
¾ cup clarified butter
¾ cup flour
2 pounds fresh spinach, finely chopped
2 cups heavy cream
3 pints shucked oysters, chopped coarse
2 tablespoons Louisiana Hot Sauce
2 tablespoons minced green onion, with some green

Melt 4 tablespoons butter over medium-high heat in a large stock pot. Add onions and celery and sauté for 5 minutes, stirring. Add Pernod and stir to deglaze the pot. Add oyster water and bring to a simmer; cook for 10 to 12 minutes, skimming occasionally. Stir in salt and pepper.

Meanwhile, combine clarified butter and flour in a heavy skillet and make a "blond roux," that is, a roux that is finished when it just begins to color instead of being dark (page 78). Add this to the hot mixture, stirring to dissolve roux. Immediately stir in spinach and allow to simmer for a few seconds. Stir in cream, oysters, and hot sauce. Simmer for about 2 minutes. Remove from heat and correct seasoning if necessary.

Serve garnished with minced green onion.

Serves 12

U N D E R T

HE TREES

New Orleans is a city of beautiful houses, marvelous food, and lively music, but one of its most spectacular attractions is its trees. You see them everywhere. ∿ First are the oaks which — some say — are hundreds of years old. Great heavy limbs swoop down to touch the ground, then curve back up to the light. Many oaks arch over the older avenues, creating telescoping views and tracing leafy patterns on old brick walks. Their gray elephant-hide trunks, limbs, and reaching roots offer deep crevices in which ferns nestle and grow. And when the spring rains come, the soaked bark turns dark as midnight, crested by a crown of glistening green. ∿ Practically as numerous as the oaks are the magnolias, dense with dark, shiny, stiff leaves — tobacco-colored underneath. Then too, there are banana trees, crepe myrtles, sweet olives, and those aloof and unexpected palms. ∿ As you drive out on the river road these varieties are joined by towering loose-limbed willows lining every canal and waterway. In mysterious still swamps are the moss-covered cypresses, knee-deep in hyacinth-crowded green water. Then, on firmer ground, the pecan groves start, and stands of pine are punctuated with catalpas clinging to moldy banks.

Left: *Pond in Audubon Park.*

SEAFOOD BOIL

Audubon Park

Boiled Crab, Crawfish,
Shrimp, Corn, and Potatoes

Remoulade Dipping Sauce

Watermelon

Beer

Iced Tea

Once part of a typically questionable land development boondoggle during Reconstruction, Audubon Park owes its present existence to the World's Industrial and Cotton Centennial Exposition of 1884–1885. On paper, the entire venture lost money, but apparently the exposition made some insiders very rich. Ultimately it was dismantled, leaving only scandal, recriminations — and the site. ✺ Until Upper City Park, as it was then known, became the site of the fair, it was a marshy lowland of tangled trees and undergrowth. Before work could commence on the pavilions, the property was cleared, drained, and filled. Then it was landscaped — after a fashion — and this was Audubon Park's real beginning. ✺ The dream, once the exposition was dismantled, was to turn the site into a beautiful city park. There were the usual years of legal maneuvering and public pleading. Then money was allocated and John C. Olmsted — nephew of Frederick Law Olmsted, (designer of New York City's Central Park) and inheritor of his famed business — accepted the commission to design the park. The project proceeded by fits and starts, but by Olmsted's death in 1920, much of the plan had been implemented and the Audubon Park we know had begun to emerge. ✺ Under the sheltering limbs of one of the park's trees we found the ideal spot to create one of the oldest feasts in New Orleans: the outdoor seafood boil.

Opposite: *Table set under the big old oaks.*

Above: *The main ingredients for a boil: crab, shrimp, and crawfish.* **Below:** *The seafood boil just ready to eat.*

Boiled Crab, Crawfish, Shrimp, Corn, and Potatoes

This brew is potent, fiery stuff — just the way they like it here. And it's designed for a big crowd.

15 quarts water
8 lemons
3 pounds onions, peeled and sliced thick
4 bags Zatarain's Seafood Boil (see Note)
3 cups coarse salt
2 cups Louisiana Hot Sauce
½ cup cayenne pepper
3 heads garlic, halved crossways
6 bay leaves
2 cups peppercorns
4 pounds small new potatoes, scrubbed and unpeeled
12 ears corn, shucked and broken in two
18 live crabs
4 pounds fresh shrimp in their shells
15 pounds live crawfish

Put the water in a 20-gallon pot. Cut the lemons in half, squeeze their juice into the water, and drop in the rinds. Add the onions and seasonings. Bring to a boil and cook for several minutes. When the boil tastes very hot and salty, it's ready.

Add the potatoes and boil for 4 to 5 minutes. Add the corn and bring back to a boil. Add the crabs and bring back to a boil. Then add the shrimp and crawfish and bring back to a final boil. Remove from the heat and let stand for 10 minutes. Drain and serve on large trays with sauces on the side.

Serves 18 to 24

Note: This is available by mail. Write to Zatarain's at 82 First Street, P.O. Box 347, Gretna, LA 70053.

Remoulade Dipping Sauce

This sauce will keep for 4 or 5 days in the refrigerator.

2 large celery ribs, chopped coarse
4 large scallions, chopped coarse, with some green
1 cup coarsely chopped parsley
2 lemon wedges (about ¼ lemon)
5 eggs
½ cup prepared horseradish
½ cup Creole mustard (see Note)
½ cup yellow mustard
1 cup catsup
¾ teaspoon salt, or to taste
4 teaspoons paprika
½ cup Worcestershire Sauce, preferably homemade (page 140)
3 cups vegetable oil
½ cup white wine vinegar

Puree the celery, scallions, parsley, and lemon wedges together in a food processor. Scrape out into a bowl and mix in eggs, horseradish, mustards, catsup, salt, paprika, and Worcestershire. Drizzle in oil, whisking to make an emulsion. Whisk in the vinegar. Correct seasoning if necessary.

Makes about 6 cups

Note: If you can't find real Creole mustard, you can substitute grainy German mustard or grainy Dijon-style mustard mixed with a bit of horseradish. The ratio I use is about ¼ teaspoon horseradish to 1 teaspoon mustard. Here, mix 2 tablespoons horseradish with 6 tablespoons grainy mustard.

From far left:
*Guesthouse. Guesthouse
and plantation bell.*
Pigeonnier. **Opposite:**
In the garden.

PICNIC UNDER THE TREES

Evergreen Plantation

Baked Quail

Molasses-Glazed Ham

Rice and Vegetable Salad

Potato Salad

Shrimp and Pasta Salad

Steamed Artichokes

Summer Fruit Pie

Pinot Noir Acacia, St. Claire, Careres 1989
Trefethen Riesling, Napa 1990

Not all the beautiful houses of the area are in New Orleans proper. A few old plantation houses still remain along the old road that curves and meanders with the Mississippi River. One such is the formally arranged complex of buildings built around a beautiful small plantation house called Evergreen. Its livable scale, only a single room deep, is one of the most appealing things about it — then there's its classic symmetry and restrained grace.

The house's most recent renovation was begun in the mid-1940s when it was purchased by the family of its present owner. One of the main changes was the rebuilding of the two graceful staircases that curve up to the second story and the enclosing of the back galleries to create long hall-like rooms on the first and second floors. All the outbuildings — the *pigeonniers,* the *garçonnières,* the classic privy, and the overseer's house — were also restored, making Evergreen one of the most complete plantation complexes in the state.

And what a place to have a picnic under the trees! Here it is.

Baked Quail

This is a quick and easy method for preparing these luscious little birds. A combination of salt and pepper could be substituted for the Creole Seasoning here.

16 partially boned quail, rib cages removed
1½ teaspoons Creole Seasoning (page 109)
1 to 2 tablespoons unsalted butter, melted

Preheat oven to 350 degrees.
  Rub quail with the seasoning and brush lightly with butter. Bake until golden, about 13 to 15 minutes.

Serves 8 or more

Molasses-Glazed Ham

Glaze
¾ cup unsulphured molasses
¼ cup white wine vinegar
2 tablespoons soy sauce
3 tablespoons cracked black pepper

1 5- to 6-pound boneless cured ham

Preheat oven to 250 degrees.
  Mix the glaze ingredients together in a small saucepan and heat. Place ham on a rack in a roasting pan. Bake for 1½ to 2 hours, basting every 10 to 15 minutes with glaze, until well glazed.
  Cool and slice thin.

Serves 18 or more

Rice and Vegetable Salad

Other vegetables could be added to this combination.

1 cup white rice
½ cup wild rice
1½ cups broccoli florets
½ cup shredded cabbage
⅓ cup thinly sliced carrots
¼ cup minced red onion
¼ cup minced Italian parsley
⅓ cup rice wine vinegar
2 tablespoons white wine vinegar
⅓ cup vegetable oil
½ teaspoon salt
½ teaspoon black pepper

Put white rice in a saucepan and cover with about 2 inches of well-salted water. Bring to a boil over high heat. Turn flame down so rice is gently boiling. Cook until tender, about 12 to 15 minutes. Drain and immediately wash with cold water. Set aside. Do the same with the wild rice, which will take slightly longer to cook. Mix the two rices together in a bowl and set aside.
  Blanch broccoli, cabbage, and carrots for 1 minute in boiling salted water. Drain and plunge into ice water. Dry and add to rice along with the red onion. Toss and set aside.
  In a small bowl, whisk all the other ingredients together and pour over rice-vegetable mixture. Toss.

Serves 8

Opposite: *Evergreen Plantation.* **Above:** *The table set for a picnic.*

Potato Salad

This is similar to German potato salad, but is served at room temperature and spiced up with Louisiana Hot Sauce.

2 pounds boiling potatoes, peeled and cut into ¾-inch dice
¼ pound thick-sliced bacon
1 large red onion, minced
1 medium green bell pepper, cut in small dice
1 tablespoon brown sugar
⅓ cup cider vinegar
¼ cup minced Italian parsley
¼ cup vegetable oil
¼ teaspoon salt
¼ teaspoon black pepper
¼ cup mayonnaise
1 teaspoon Louisiana Hot Sauce
4 hard-cooked eggs, chopped coarse
5 green onions, sliced

Cover potatoes with well-salted water and bring quickly to a boil over high heat; turn flame down so water is just boiling lightly. Cook until tender, about 11 to 12 minutes. Drain, wash with cold water, and drain again. Set aside.

Fry bacon in a skillet until golden and remove with a slotted spoon to drain. Pour out all but 2 or 3 tablespoons of the fat and sauté onions and green pepper for a minute, over medium heat. Add brown sugar and vinegar, and stir over heat to dissolve the sugar.

Place the potatoes in a bowl, pour in the skillet mixture, and toss lightly. Mix parsley, oil, salt, pepper, mayonnaise, and hot sauce. Add this and the bacon; toss again lightly. Garnish with the eggs and green onion.

Serves 8

Shrimp and Pasta Salad

Tiny green peas are also good in this.

1 pound shell pasta
2½ cups cold water
1 lemon
½ teaspoon red pepper flakes
2 medium bay leaves
1 tablespoon salt
1 tablespoon paprika
½ teaspoon chili powder
½ pound raw medium shrimp, peeled and deveined
¼ cup catsup
1 cup mayonnaise
2 tablespoons rice wine vinegar
⅓ cup diced pineapple
1 teaspoon Louisiana Hot Sauce
⅓ cup diced red bell pepper
⅓ cup diced green bell pepper
⅓ cup diced red onion
¼ cup minced Italian parsley
¼ teaspoon salt
¼ teaspoon black pepper

Cook pasta according to package directions. Drain, rinse in cold water, and set aside.

In a saucepan, bring 2½ cups water to a boil. Cut the lemon in half. Squeeze in the juice and drop in the rinds. Add pepper flakes, bay leaves, salt, paprika, and chili powder. Simmer for 3 minutes, then add the shrimp. When water comes back to a boil, remove from flame and allow shrimp to rest in the water for 5 minutes. Drain, cool, and cut shrimp in half. Toss with the pasta.

In a small bowl, combine catsup, mayonnaise, vinegar, pineapple, and hot sauce. Toss in with pasta-shrimp mixture. Toss in peppers, onion, parsley, salt, and pepper. Adjust seasoning if necessary. Chill before serving.

Serves 8

Steamed Artichokes

You could use any kind of dipping sauce you like with these. We used a garlic mayonnaise.

8 medium artichokes, with ¼ inch cut off bottoms and ¾ inch cut off tops
3 quarts water
2 tablespoons salt
½ lemon, squeezed, with shell reserved
2 tablespoons vinegar

Remove tough outer leaves from artichokes and trim pointed top off all remaining leaves. Put in a large pot and cover with other ingredients, including reserved half lemon shell. Bring to a boil over high heat, turn down to a slow boil, and cook until tender (the point of a knife will easily pierce the bottom of an artichoke), about 30 minutes. Drain and cool, inverted, on a towel.

Serves 8

Garlic Mayonnaise

2 whole medium heads of garlic, top ¼ inch sliced off
2 teaspoons olive oil
Pinch of salt
Pinch of black pepper
2 cups mayonnaise
3 tablespoons fresh lemon juice (1 lemon)
¼ teaspoon salt
¼ teaspoon white pepper

Preheat oven to 275 degrees.

Place garlic heads in a small pan lined with foil. Drizzle oil over each and sprinkle with salt and pepper. Bake until tender, 45 minutes or more.

Peel and puree the roasted garlic. Combine the puree with the other ingredients. Chill.

Makes about 2 cups

Summer Fruit Pie

This is a marvelous combination of fruit for a pie.

Pastry

2¼ cups flour
½ teaspoon salt
¾ cup unsalted butter, chilled and cut into bits
¼ cup ice water

Filling

2 ripe peaches, skinned, stoned, and cut into
  ½-inch slices
2 nectarines, skinned, stoned, and cut into
  ½-inch slices
2 large red plums, skinned, stoned, and cut into
  ½-inch slices
12 large strawberries, halved
12 bing cherries, stoned
½ cup plus 1 tablespoon sugar
1 tablespoon quick-cooking tapioca
Milk

Make the pastry: Stir together the flour and salt. Quickly cut in the butter with two knives or a pastry blender until the mixture resembles coarse meal. Sprinkle with the ice water and mix lightly. Form into a flat disc, wrap in plastic, and refrigerate for at least half an hour.

Finish the pie: Preheat oven to 450 degrees.

Divide pastry in half. Roll out one piece ¼ inch thcikon a floured surface and line a 9-inch pie pan. Place all the fruit in a bowl and toss with the ½ cup sugar and tapioca. Heap into pie pan.

Roll out remaining pastry to ¼ inch thick and place on top of fruit. Trim, seal, and crimp. Brush top crust with a small amount of milk, vent it, and sprinkle with the remaining tablespoon of sugar. Bake 15 minutes. Reduce heat to 350 degrees and bake for another 30 minutes, until top is golden. Cool before serving.

Serves 8 or more

Below left: *Summer Fruit Pie.* **Below right:** *Live oaks.*

O W N

In New Orleans "Uptown" means everything above Canal Street. It's where the Garden District with its splendid architecture is and where the universities are. Serene Audubon Park and the Zoo are both uptown. St. Charles Avenue cuts right through uptown's middle. With the wild celebration that grips the city with Mardi Gras frenzy, St. Charles becomes a fantasy street. Otherwise it's calmer; the streetcar rocks breezily up from Canal, windows thrown open for most of the year, finally turning around deep into Carrolton Avenue for the trip back. ∾ Over toward the river, new life is coming to old neighborhoods. The warehouses along the river are being converted to other, more diverse uses. And Magazine Street has sprouted shops of all kinds — less expensive versions of the Royal Street emporiums and whimsical little places that sell whatever their owners dream of. ∾ But back around the streets just off the spine of the trolley route, avenues are shaded by excellent old oaks with roots that make the sidewalks crack and heave. The great houses doze in the relentless heat of summer and all looks serene and almost timeless. ∾ Maybe it really is what it seems, a dream of the past — perpetuated for us today.

Left: *Audubon Park.*

SUMPTUOUS PICNIC FOOD

Brevard-Rice House

Seafood Stuffed Artichokes

Oyster Salad with Radish Relish

Jalapeño Corn Bread Sticks

Paprika Twists

Tomato Bread

Gingered Carrot Torte with Rum Sauce

Chocolate Layer Cake

Lemon Cake

Penfolds "Barrel Fermented" Chardonnay, South Australia 1987

Don't panic when you look at this menu. We're not trying to overwork you — quite the opposite. This terrace was so inviting and shady that we decided to do a big mix-and-match group of dishes. Everything is pretty portable and will travel from kitchen to terrace or patio or deck, and you can make any combination you find appealing. Plus, you can add to or subtract from the garnishes to suit your mood or time. ∾ To go with the seafood are three different kinds of breads—all equally tasty. To finish, we have one spectacular gingered carrot torte and two very fine layer cakes that will serve you well for any occasion. As I've said, these are flexible meals. What we have presented here is what we consider the best of all possible combinations — everything!

Above: *Seafood Stuffed Artichokes.* **Opposite:** *Brevard-Rice House.*

Above: *Table set by the pool.* **Below:** *Back garden.*

Seafood Stuffed Artichokes

These taste as good as they look.

6 large artichokes, stem and top inch of leaves cut off
1 large lemon, cut in half
2 tablespoons salt
2 bay leaves
1 cup Shallot Vinaigrette (recipe follows)

Stuffing
36 small shrimp, cooked and peeled
½ pound jumbo lump crabmeat, picked over
½ pound poached firm-fleshed fish such as tuna or
    trout, broken into medium pieces (see Note)
2 carrots, scraped and cut into 3 by ⅛-inch julienne
2 small yellow squash, trimmed, seeded, and julienned
    as above
2 small zucchini squash, trimmed, seeded, and julienned
    as above
1 medium onion, cut in thin strips lengthwise
1½ cups Shallot Vinaigrette (recipe follows)
Salt and pepper to taste

Place trimmed artichokes in a large pot. Pour in
enough water to just cover. Remove artichokes and
set aside. Squeeze the lemon halves into water and
drop them in, add salt and bay leaves; cover and
bring to a boil over high heat. Drop in the
artichokes, and weight them with a plate to keep
them submerged. Boil gently over medium low heat
until tender (test by piercing bottom with a sharp
knife; the knife should meet with a little resistance),
about 15 minutes. Do not overcook. Drain the
artichokes, refresh them in ice water, then drain
upside down on a towel. Remove the choke from the
artichokes and discard. Place artichokes right side up
and pour the vinaigrette over them. Reserve.

Make the stuffing: Combine all the ingredients and
toss gently. Add salt and pepper if desired.

To serve, stuff the cavities of the artichokes. Then,
working outward, separate the leaves and stuff more
of the mixture in between them, forcing the leaves
out like petals of a flower.

Serves 6

Note: You may simply place fish fillets in a shallow baking
dish. Sprinkle in some herbs, a squeeze of lemon, salt and
pepper, then pour a mixture of white wine and water. Cover
with foil and bake in a 350-degree oven until flaky, about 10
minutes. Or you could poach it in a traditional court-
bouillon. Or you could substitute lobster or more crabmeat.

Shallot Vinaigrette
¾ cup white wine vinegar
1¾ cups olive oil
1 teaspoon salt
1 teaspoon white pepper
1 tablespoon minced basil or thyme
1 teaspoon minced shallots
1 teaspoon minced garlic

Whisk together the vinegar, oil, salt, and pepper.
Stir in the herb, shallots, and garlic. Refrigerate.

Makes 2½ cups

Above: *Canna lily.*

ABOUT THE HOUSE

Here's a rarity. We know the name of the person who caused the house to be built: Albert Hamilton Brevard; we know the name of the architect who designed it: James Carlow; the date the contract was signed: 3 January 1857; the price: $13,000; and even the name of the builder: Charles Pride.

For his $13,000 Brevard got a two-story Greek Revival house with attic. The double galleries are supported by "columns in antae," Corinthian and Ionic columns placed between square pilasters. A recessed entrance provides space for a pair of massive storm doors that can be folded back from the front portal. All downstairs rooms are ornamented with elaborate plasterwork on the cornices and central medallions. Each parlor has a marble mantel, one depicting spring and the other autumn. The many windows that open onto the galleries and balconies were all fitted with handmade glass.

On the south side of the house are a hexagonal library with bedroom above and two more galleries with delicate ironwork which duplicates that on the front balustrades. These were added in the 1860s by the Emory Clapps.

Over the years, through several changes of ownership, those occupying the house all seemed to have been keenly interested in the garden. Soaring boxwood, cherry laurels, sweet olives, camellias, japonicas, and azaleas surround the terrace, and blooming vines have woven into the decorative grillwork, creating a secluded retreat.

Oyster Salad with Radish Relish

You could substitute large shrimp or crawfish tails for the oysters and come up with a tasty variation.

Oysters
36 freshly shucked oysters, drained
¼ cup Creole Seasoning (page 109)
1 cup flour
1 cup masa harina
Oil for deep-frying

Assembly
1 medium head radicchio, cleaned and torn into
   bite-size pieces
1 medium head green leaf lettuce, cleaned and torn into
   bite-size pieces
Roasted Garlic Dressing (recipe follows)
36 medium asparagus spears, trimmed and blanched
   for 2 minutes
12 Belgian endive leaves
Radish Relish (recipe follows)

Fry the oysters: Sprinkle the oysters with 3 tablespoons of Creole Seasoning. Set aside. Toss together the flour, masa harina, and remaining Creole Seasoning.

Heat the oil in a deep fryer to 350 degrees. Dredge the oysters in the flour mixture, coating them well and shaking off the excess. Fry until golden, about 2 to 3 minutes. Drain on paper towels.

Assemble the salad: Toss the greens with enough of the Roasted Garlic Dressing to coat. Arrange on 6 large plates. Top each salad with 6 oysters and garnish with asparagus, endive, and Radish Relish. Drizzle a bit more of the garlic dressing over all and serve immediately.

Serves 6

Note: You might want to make the salad before you fry the oysters, because the sooner you eat the oysters, the better you'll like them.

Opposite left: *Recessed front entrance.* **Opposite right:** *Athena amid the garden begonias.*

Roasted Garlic Dressing
20 medium garlic cloves, peeled
2 cups olive oil
2 egg yolks
2 teaspoons Dijon-style mustard
2 teaspoons minced anchovy
½ cup white wine vinegar
½ teaspoon salt
¼ teaspoon white pepper
1 tablespoon fresh lemon juice
1 tablespoon minced parsley

Preheat oven to 300 degrees.

Place garlic in a small ovenproof dish and cover with the olive oil, making sure cloves are submerged. Cover with foil and bake until garlic is soft and begins to color, about 1 hour. Allow to cool. Strain out garlic cloves and reserve garlic and oil separately.

Place garlic, yolks, mustard, anchovy, and vinegar in the bowl of a food processor and puree for 30 seconds. With the machine running, pour in 1½ cups of the reserved olive oil in a thin steady stream. Stir in salt, pepper, and lemon juice. Check for seasoning and stir in parsley.

Makes 3 cups

Radish Relish
¾ cup finely chopped radishes
1 teaspoon minced shallots
1 teaspoon minced garlic
1 tablespoon whole capers
2 tablespoons olive oil
½ teaspoon salt
¼ teaspoon white pepper

Mix all ingredients together. Cover and allow to marinate overnight in the refrigerator.

Makes 1 scant cup

Jalapeño Corn Bread Sticks

These would be good with almost anything!

⅓ cup vegetable oil
1 egg
1¼ cups milk
1 tablespoon Louisiana Hot Sauce
1 cup yellow cornmeal
1 cup all-purpose flour
1 tablespoon baking powder
1 teaspoon salt
2 tablespoons minced jalapeño pepper
1 tablespoon minced red bell pepper
1 tablespoon minced green onion, green part only

Preheat oven to 375 degrees and grease corn stick pans.

Mix together the oil, egg, milk, and hot sauce in a large mixing bowl. Stir in the other ingredients in the order listed. Do not overmix. Spoon into corn stick pans. Bake until golden, about 12 to 15 minutes.

Makes 12

Paprika Twists

These are marvelous looking and very light.

1 10 x 15-inch sheet of puff pastry
½ cup milk
1 egg
1 cup grated Romano cheese
¼ cup paprika
1 tablespoon cayenne pepper

Preheat oven to 350 degrees.

Lay pastry on a flat surface. Beat milk and egg together and brush pastry liberally with it. Mix cheese, paprika, and cayenne together and sprinkle half on top of the coated pastry. Turn the pastry over, brush with the egg wash, and sprinkle with the balance of the cheese mixture. Cut pastry into 1 x 10-inch strips. Pick up each strip by one end, twist it several times, and lay on a parchment-lined baking sheet. Bake for 15 to 20 minutes. Cool on a rack.

Makes 15 twists

Tomato Bread

I think this would be mighty good with soup.

2 packages active dry yeast
1½ cups warm water, about 110 degrees
7¼ cups flour
2 tablespoons olive oil
1¼ cups diced red onion
1 jalapeño pepper, seeded and minced
1 cup roasted, seeded, and diced red bell pepper
½ pound plum tomatoes, peeled, seeded, and chopped fine
15 basil leaves, cut into thin strips
½ teaspoon salt
½ teaspoon white pepper

Dissolve yeast in the water and stir in ¼ cup of flour. Set aside. Heat oil in a skillet over a medium flame and sauté onion and pepper until they begin to soften, about 2 or 3 minutes. Add red pepper, tomatoes, basil, salt, and pepper and cook for another 2 or 3 minutes. Scrape this into a large bowl and allow to cool for 10 to 15 minutes.

Add yeast mixture to the vegetables and mix. Stir in the flour a cup at a time until you get a kneadable dough — you may not need the entire 7 cups. Turn dough out onto a floured surface and knead lightly, just enough to form into a ball. Put ball into an oiled bowl and turn to oil all sides. Cover with plastic wrap and allow to double in bulk, about 1 hour. Punch down again and transfer to a floured surface again and roll out into a 12 x 15-inch rectangle. Divide in half along the 12-inch axis. Roll each jelly-roll fashion to make two 12-inch loaves. Place loaves onto a parchment-lined baking sheet. Cover lightly and allow to rise again, about 35 to 40 minutes.

Preheat oven to 350 degrees.

Bake until lightly browned, about 25 to 30 minutes. Cool on a rack.

Makes 2 loaves

Opposite: *Jalapeño Corn Bread Sticks, Paprika Twists, and Tomato Bread.*

Gingered Carrot Torte
with Rum Sauce

*The sauce that goes with this really
enhances the torte's flavor, so don't skip it if
you can avoid doing so.*

5 eggs

1¾ cups vegetable oil

3 cups scraped and grated carrots

½ cup grated ginger

2¼ cups sugar

1 teaspoon cinnamon

1¾ cups chopped toasted pecans

2 cups unsifted flour

2½ teaspoons baking powder

1 teaspoon salt

Rum Sauce

½ cup granulated sugar

1 cup brown sugar, tightly packed

½ cup lime juice

½ cup dark rum

3 tablespoons unsalted butter

Preheat oven to 325 degrees.

Butter a 10-inch cake pan and line the bottom with a round of parchment. Butter and then flour the whole thing, shaking out any excess flour.

With a mixer at slow speed, beat together the eggs, oil, carrots, and ginger until well combined. Stir together the sugar, cinnamon, and pecans. Add this to the carrot mixture, combining well. Sift together the flour, baking powder, and salt. Add this to the batter and mix well. Scrape into the prepared pan. Bake until center bounces back when touched, about 35 to 40 minutes. Cool on a rack.

Make the sauce: Combine the sugars, lime juice, and rum in a small saucepan and warm over low heat until the sugars are melted. Divide this mixture into 2 portions and stir the butter into one of them.

Run a knife around the edges of the torte to loosen it. Turn out onto a rack and peel off the parchment. Flip the torte onto a serving dish and glaze with the buttered sauce. Pour the reserved sauce into a sauceboat and serve on the side.

Serves 8 to 12

Chocolate Layer Cake

You can't have too many chocolate cake recipes.

2¼ cups cake flour
¾ teaspoon baking powder
¾ teaspoon baking soda
1½ cups milk
7 ounces semisweet chocolate, chopped fine
6 ounces unsalted butter, softened
2 cups sugar
4 eggs
1 teaspoon vanilla extract
Chocolate Frosting (recipe follows)

Preheat oven to 350 degrees.

Butter two 8-inch cake pans. Line bottoms with parchment and butter the parchment. Flour insides of both and shake out any excess.

Sift together the flour, baking powder, and soda. Set aside. Bring milk to a slow boil over medium heat in a medium saucepan. Add chocolate and stir until melted. Set aside. Cream butter and sugar together until light and fluffy. Beat in eggs, one at a time, then the vanilla. Add flour mixture and chocolate mixture alternately, mixing well after each addition. Pour into prepared pans and bake until tester comes out clean, about 35 minutes. Cool in pans and turn out. Slice off rounded top of each layer. Slice each layer in two to make 4 thin layers.

Put layers together with the frosting, holding them in place with toothpicks as you assemble the cake. Frost outsides and refrigerate until ready to serve. Cut with a warm knife.

Serves 8 to 12

Chocolate Frosting

3 cups heavy cream
2 tablespoons unsalted butter
1 pound semisweet chocolate, chopped fine

Combine cream and butter in a saucepan and bring to a boil over medium heat, stirring, until butter is melted and mixture is smooth. Remove from heat and stir in chocolate until chocolate is melted. Refrigerate to cool. Chill a mixing bowl and pour mixture in. Whip with a hand mixer until frosting forms soft peaks. Do not overmix.

Lemon Cake

This is another one you can't have too many recipes for.

Zest of 2 lemons
1 cup sugar
1 cup unsalted butter, softened
3 eggs
1½ cups all-purpose flour
1 teaspoon baking powder
½ teaspoon salt
6 tablespoons fresh lemon juice
2 teaspoons vanilla extract
Lemon Frosting (recipe follows)

Preheat oven to 350 degrees.

Butter two 8-inch cake pans and line bottoms with parchment paper. Butter the paper and flour both pans, shaking out excess. Set aside.

Combine zest and sugar in the bowl of a food processor and pulse until finely ground. Combine this with the butter and beat with a hand mixer until light and fluffy. Beat in eggs one at a time. Sift together the dry ingredients and mix lemon juice with the vanilla. Add dry ingredients to the butter mixture, alternating with the liquids, mixing well. Pour into prepared pans and bake until top springs back to the touch and a tester comes out clean, about 40 minutes. Let cool and turn layers out. Slice each layer in two to make 4 thin layers, and frost with Lemon Frosting.

Serves 8 to 12

Lemon Frosting

Zest and juice from 1 lemon
¾ cup sugar
2¼ pounds cream cheese, at room temperature

Process zest and sugar as above in a food processor and beat in with the cream cheese and lemon juice until smooth. You may do this all in the processor if you like. Chill for about an hour before using.

Note: When we made our chocolate and lemon cakes, we baked them in single deep pans and sliced them into 3 layers.

Above: *Gingered Carrot Torte with Rum Sauce, Lemon Cake, and Chocolate Layer Cake.* **Below:** *Chair in front of a lace-curtained window.*

ANOTHER SEAFOOD SUPPER

de Saulles-White House

Smoked Fish Cakes with Caper Sauce

Grilled Pompano with Thyme and Garlic Butter

Vegetable Lasagna

Green Salad

Sour Cream Pecan Cake with Fresh Peaches, Peach Coulis, and Whipped Cream

Ferrari Carano "Reserve" Chardonnay, Alexander Valley 1988

Crescent City residents are so accustomed to the bounty of the Gulf, with its regular outpouring of all sorts of fish and seafood, that they seem to like nothing better than serving it for several courses. Early city menus reveal that diners often began with assorted oyster dishes and fish-based soup, then went on to feast on fish stuffed with more seafood and served with a seafood sauce. This proclivity is evident in the menu, in which two different kinds of fish are served. ∾ It begins with luscious, smoked fish cakes in a light caper sauce. Grilled pompano just brushed with thyme and garlic butter follows. The vegetable accompaniment is called a vegetable lasagna. By whatever name, this dish is an uncomplicated mix of good flavorful summer vegetables and I'm sure you'll be able to put this to many other uses. For instance, it would be perfect for a vegetarian meal. With the addition of a few shrimp or crawfish, it could be a light main course in itself. ∾ After the green salad, there's a dessert of sour cream pecan cake with sliced peaches and peach coulis, a winning combination.

Above: *Vine-crowned doorway to the greenhouses.* **Opposite:** *Grilled Pompano with Thyme and Garlic Butter.*

ABOUT THE HOUSE

Louis de Saulles, the first owner of the property, was born in Middlesex County, England, and was probably drawn to New Orleans as many others were during the city's boom years in the early part of the nineteenth century. Apparently he was well connected and made a "good" marriage in 1836 to Mlle. Armide Longer, daughter of a prominent Creole family.

The wealthy families in New Orleans almost all had close European connections in those early days and were accustomed to traveling back and forth between the South, New York, and Europe. So it was that by 1856 the de Saulleses had resettled and were living in New York City, and the house was sold in that same year. In the intervening years the property has had nineteen known ownerships, included among them some

of New Orleans's more notable families.

Remarkably, the de Saulles-White House is today very much as it was when first constructed. Unlike some of its contemporaries, the house didn't go through the cycle of fashionable face-lifts and haphazard additions. Maybe its classic simplicity was strong enough to dissuade any would-be tinkers. Whatever, the front facade has changed little, and its basic massive shape, faced on both ends by beautifully symmetrical rows of square columns, is as it was originally designed and built. The great urns on their heavy square pedestals came later, by 1894 (as evidenced by a sketch of the house with that date). This addition reflected the Italianate taste of the time, but if anything, they enhance the beauty of the house.

Smoked Fish Cakes with Caper Sauce

This is another of those first courses that could easily become a main course. You might want to use a fruit salsa with it instead of the Caper Sauce called for here.

20 to 24 ounces smoked white fish, such as mahi mahi
1½ teaspoons Creole Seasoning (recipe follows)
1 tablespoon Creole mustard (see Note, page 87)
3 tablespoons mayonnaise
1 teaspoon chopped capers
2 tablespoons chopped green onion tops
1 egg
2 tablespoons dried bread crumbs
¼ teaspoon salt
¼ teaspoon white pepper
Caper Sauce (recipe follows)

Preheat oven to 350 degrees.

Crumble fish, discarding any skin or bones, into small chunks (do not crumble too fine). In a small bowl mix together the Creole Seasoning, mustard, mayonnaise, capers, and green onion. Add fish and mix lightly. Break the egg over mixture. Sprinkle bread crumbs, salt, and pepper over all and mix lightly with your hands. Form into 6 cakes about 2 inches in diameter and 1 inch thick. Do not compress; just pat together.

Place on an ungreased baking sheet and bake for 10 to 12 minutes, until set and just barely beginning to turn color.

Serve hot from the oven with Caper Sauce.

Makes 6

Creole Seasoning

⅓ cup salt
¼ cup granulated or powdered garlic (see Note)
¼ cup freshly ground black pepper
2 teaspoons cayenne pepper
2 teaspoons dried thyme
2 teaspoons dried oregano
⅓ teaspoon paprika
1 tablespoon granulated or powdered onion (see Note)

Combine all ingredients in a food processor. Whirl around for about 15 seconds to mix well. Store in a tightly sealed jar.

Makes 2 cups

Note: Be sure that you select the brands that don't contain MSG.

Caper Sauce

1 teaspoon vegetable oil
2 tablespoons minced red onion
1 garlic clove, minced
¼ cup white wine vinegar
2 cups heavy cream
1 tablespoon chopped parsley
1 tablespoon capers, rinsed
Salt and white pepper to taste

Heat the oil in a medium saucepan over medium-high heat. Add the onion and garlic and sauté until translucent. Add the vinegar and reduce to about 1 tablespoon. Then add the cream and reduce to about one cup.

Remove from the heat, stir in parsley and capers, and salt and pepper to taste.

Makes about 1 cup

Opposite: *The de Saulles-White house.* **Above left:** *The table and Smoked Fish Cakes with Caper Sauce.*

Above left: *Living room corner.* **Above right:** *Flowers on the mantelpiece.* **Below:** *Green Salad.* **Opposite:** *Double dolphin fountain.*

Grilled Pompano with Thyme and Garlic Butter

Any firm, mild, white fish may be substituted.

6 pompano fillets, about 5 to 6 ounces each
1 teaspoon salt
½ teaspoon black pepper
Olive oil
½ cup (1 stick) unsalted butter
1½ tablespoons finely minced garlic
1 tablespoon Worcestershire sauce
Juice of 2 lemons
1 teaspoon salt
1½ tablespoons coarsely chopped fresh thyme
½ teaspoon white pepper
Pan-Roasted Shallots (recipe follows), optional

Preheat grill or broiler for at least 20 minutes.

Lay fillets out on a tray. Mix together the salt and black pepper and rub the fish with it.

Brush the grill or broiler with a little olive oil and cook fish about 1½ to 2 minutes per side, depending on thickness, until it is just beginning to flake.

Meanwhile (or before you start the fish), melt butter in a medium skillet over high heat. Add garlic, stirring and continuing to cook until garlic just begins to brown lightly, about 1 minute. Add Worcestershire sauce, lemon juice, and salt. The mixture should be a light caramel color. Add thyme and remove from heat. Stir in pepper.

Brush fish lightly with the infused butter as it is served. Garnish with Pan-Roasted Shallots.

Serves 6

Pan-Roasted Shallots
1 tablespoon olive oil
16 medium shallots, peeled
¼ teaspoon salt
¼ teaspoon white pepper

Preheat oven to 275 degrees.

Heat oil in an ovenproof skillet over medium-high heat. Add shallots, salt, and pepper, and toss. Cook, stirring, until shallots begin to brown slightly and caramelize. Bake in oven until very tender, about 10 to 15 minutes.

Vegetable Lasagna

Here is that delicious little concoction I
mentioned in the introduction. All the vegetables
should be thinly sliced, but they don't have to
be peeled. A mandoline is handy here.

1 medium eggplant, trimmed and thinly sliced lengthwise
4 medium onions, peeled and thinly sliced
¾ teaspoon salt
¾ teaspoon white pepper
1 tablespoon minced garlic
6 medium green zucchini, trimmed and thinly sliced
   lengthwise
8 ripe tomatoes, thinly sliced
1 cup grated Parmesan cheese
1 to 1½ tablespoons minced parsley

Preheat oven to 325 degrees.
  Generously oil the bottom and sides of an 8 x
10-inch gratin dish. Cover the bottom of the dish
with slightly overlapping eggplant slices. Top this
with a layer of slightly overlapping onion slices.
Sprinkle with ¼ teaspoon each of salt and pepper
and some of the garlic. Layer the zucchini, then
tomatoes, and then again zucchini. Season again as
above. Press down with your hand to compact the
layers. Put on another layer of slightly overlapping
tomatoes and finish with a layer of eggplant and the
final seasoning. Sprinkle cheese and parsley over all.
Cover with foil and bake for 15 minutes. Remove
foil and bake until lightly brown, about another 10
to 15 minutes. Remove from oven and pour off
excess liquid. Serve either warm or at room
temperature.

Serves 6 or more

Green Salad

Whatever combination of greens you favor would be fine for this. The salad should be a small one for this menu.

6 to 8 cups mixed greens, washed and dried
3 thin slices red onion, separated into rings and cut in
    half
3 tablespoons olive oil
1 tablespoon vegetable oil
1 tablespoon white wine vinegar
Salt and pepper to taste

Toss greens in a bowl with the onion. Whisk together all other ingredients and spoon enough over greens, tossing to coat leaves. Serve with melba toast or a round of toasted French bread.

Serves 6

Sour Cream Pecan Cake with Fresh Peaches, Peach Coulis, and Whipped Cream

Obviously, you could substitute ice cream or vanilla sauce for the whipped cream here. Or, heaven forbid, do without.

1 cup (2 sticks) unsalted butter, softened
2 ¾ cups sugar
2 eggs
2½ cups sour cream
1 tablespoon vanilla extract
2 cups flour
1 tablespoon baking powder
¼ teaspoon salt
2 cups chopped toasted pecans
1 tablespoon cinnamon
Fresh Peaches and Peach Coulis (recipe follows)
Whipped cream

Preheat oven to 350 degrees.
  Grease and flour a 10-inch tube pan. Set aside.
  Cream the butter and 2 cups of the sugar until light and fluffy, about 3 minutes. Add eggs, beating until well mixed. Mix in sour cream and vanilla, combining well. Sift together the flour, baking

Opposite: *Sour Cream Pecan Cake with Fresh Peaches, Peach Coulis, and Whipped Cream.* **Above:** *Chairs against the painted dining room wall.*

powder, and salt. Sprinkle over the other mixture and combine well.
  Pour half the batter (it will be stiff) into the prepared pan. Toss together pecans, remaining sugar, and cinnamon and sprinkle over the batter in pan. Top with the balance of the batter and smooth top. Bake for 1 hour, or until a cake tester comes out clean.
  Serve with Fresh Peaches and Peach Coulis and a big dollop of whipped cream.

Serves 8 to 12

Fresh Peaches and Peach Coulis
10 ripe peaches, skinned and pitted
1 to 1½ cups sugar, depending on sweetness of the fruit
¼ cup peach schnapps
2 tablespoons peach brandy or regular brandy
1 cup heavy cream
Vanilla extract to taste

Slice 4 of the peaches, sprinkle with sugar, and set aside. Place remaining peaches, sugar to taste, schnapps, and brandy into a food processor and puree.
  Whip cream to soft peaks and sweeten if desired. Flavor with a little vanilla, schnapps, and/or brandy.
  Refrigerate.

Makes about 6 cups

A NEW OLD FAVORITE

Grima House

Crab with Ravigote Sauce

Trout in a Shoestring Potato Crust

Bread Pudding Soufflé with Whiskey Sauce

Joseph Drouhin Pouille-Fuissé 1990

Those of you who are familiar with the Crescent City and its people probably already know how much they value tradition. You also probably know how much they like fun. Well, I think this simple little menu expresses both these aspects of the city's personality. The meal begins with lump crabmeat, a delicacy that has been a tradition for as long as crabs have been hauled in by Gulf fishermen. Crabmeat is enjoyed in many ways, but probably none is better than served on a bed of greens with a mayonnaise dressing like the ravigote sauce here. That's the tradition. The fun comes from trout fillets that are coated with shoestring potatoes before being gently sautéed. I guess you could almost say this is the local version of fish and chips. The fillets rest on a slick of fresh tomato coulis with a sprinkling of caramelized onions. Fun, but no laughing matter. It's easy too. This brings us to dessert. In this city known for its bread puddings someone was bound to come up with a bread pudding soufflé. I can't imagine a better version than the one here, gilded with whiskey sauce.

Opposite: *Shuttered windows in the front facade.*

ABOUT THE HOUSE

Grima House had a rather turbulent beginning.
The house was probably built by a Cornelius
Bicknell Payne some time between 1857 and
1861. Records show that the house changed
hands in '61 and was sold again soon after. The
new owner was Alfred Grima, who gave the place
his name. Grima hired the architect Paul Audrey
to remodel, but died only five days after
contracting for the work. His wife, Emma, went
forward with the plans.

Audrey designed the large-scale Baroque
ornamentation that gives the house its special
character. He put the arches over the corner
pilasters and the anthemion finial on the peaked
roof. By the time he was done, the house had
been transformed into a modified French château
typical of New Orleans residential architecture in
the late 1800s. In the 1920s, Mrs. Grima engaged
Charles R. Armstrong to design a formal garden
— the first such along St. Charles Avenue to be
landscaped in a modern manner.

When Alfred, Jr., married, he and his new
bride, Clarisse, moved into the house with his
mother. There all three lived — by all accounts
in harmony — until only Clarisse remained. She
sold the house, but missed it enough to
repurchase it, and she lived out her remaining
years there.

The property was bequeathed to the Historic
New Orleans Collection, from which the present
owners purchased it. They seem as devoted to it
as any of the Grimas were, ensuring that this
beautiful and tranquil place will sail serenely
into the next century.

Above: Grima House. **Below left:** *Entrance pediment detail.*
Below center: *The boxwood garden.* **Below right:** *Crab with
Ravigote Sauce.* **Overleaf:** *A tapestry-covered English chair
at left and an unusual brass newel post at right.*

Crab with Ravigote Sauce

*Another way to serve New Orleans back
fin lump crabmeat is to place a scoop of it in the
center of a plate, surround that with slices of Creole
tomatoes and hard-cooked eggs, and dress it with
homemade mayonnaise and lemon wedges.*

1 cup mayonnaise, preferably homemade
⅓ cup Creole mustard (see Note, page 87)
¼ cup prepared horseradish, drained
1 generous tablespoon minced green onion, with some
    green
1 tablespoon finely minced parsley
1 hard-cooked egg, finely chopped
1 tablespoon lemon juice
1½ teaspoons minced capers, plus extra whole ones for
    garnish
4 or more cups mixed salad greens, cut into thin strips
3 cups back fin lump crabmeat, picked over
1 lemon, cut into 6 wedges

Mix mayonnaise, mustard, and horseradish well,
then add all other ingredients except whole capers,
salad greens, crabmeat, and lemon wedges. Mix it
all well.

To assemble, place shredded greens on individual
plates with a serving of crabmeat in the center of
each. Top with sauce and a sprinkling of whole
capers and garnish each with a lemon wedge.

Serves 6

Above: *Trout in a Shoestring Potato Crust.* **Below:** *Venetian armchair.* **Right:** *Silver behind the sofa.*

Trout in a Shoestring Potato Crust

This method works with any kind of firm fish fillet.

6 trout fillets, 4 to 5 ounces each
2 teaspoons salt
1 teaspoon white pepper
1 cup flour
8 cups shredded or shoestring potatoes (about 6 medium)
¾ cup olive oil
Tomato Coulis (recipe follows)
Caramelized Onions (recipe follows)
4 pieces pickled okra, cut into rings (optional)
1 lemon, cut into wedges (optional)

Lay fillets out on a sheet of waxed paper. Mix salt and pepper and sprinkle the fish. Mix leftover salt and pepper with the flour. Dredge fillets well in the flour and shake off excess. Place on a plate and cover lightly with waxed paper. Refrigerate for at least 30 minutes.

Put shredded potatoes in a shallow bowl and carefully place each fillet on them, pressing down to make potatoes adhere on both sides — don't worry, it will look messy. (During refrigeration, the flour will have combined with moisture from the fish, making its surface sticky.) Put each coated fillet aside on a tray as it is finished.

Heat oil in a very large skillet over a high flame. When very hot, carefully place 3 fillets in the pan, skin side down. Turn the heat down slightly and allow to cook undisturbed for a minute or two. Beginning with the two ends, gently slide a spatula under the cooking fillets to loosen any points that may be sticking; after about 3 minutes, lift an end to check that they are not browning too quickly. When golden, 4 to 6 minutes, turn carefully and repeat the process. Before turning, you may sprinkle a few more shredded potatoes on top and press them down lightly. Hold the potatoes in place with your hand while you turn the fish with the spatula.

Add more oil if necessary to cook the second batch.

To serve, spread a generous slick of Tomato Coulis on individual plates and sprinkle with Caramelized Onions. Top with a fillet and garnish with rings of pickled okra and a lemon wedge.

Serves 6

Fresh Tomato Coulis

Of course this would make a delightful summer pasta sauce, with or without the addition of fresh basil or tarragon.

¼ cup olive oil
1 generous tablespoon minced garlic
5 cups peeled, seeded, and pureed ripe tomatoes
1 teaspoon salt
½ teaspoon black pepper
2 medium ripe tomatoes, peeled, seeded, and chopped
2 tablespoons finely minced parsley
1 teaspoon white wine vinegar

Heat oil in a saucepan over medium heat. Add garlic, cook for a minute, or until softened but not browned. Add tomato puree, salt, and pepper. Bring to a boil, stirring occasionally, and turn heat to low. Continue to cook, stirring occasionally, for another 10 to 12 minutes. Add chopped tomatoes and cook an additional 5 minutes, stirring occasionally, until sauce is thickened. Stir in parsley and vinegar.

Makes about 4 cups

Caramelized Onions

3 tablespoons olive oil
3 medium onions, halved and sliced
1 teaspoon salt
Pinch of white pepper

Heat oil in a large skillet over a medium-high flame until very hot. Add onions and stir to coat. Add salt and pepper and continue to cook, stirring occasionally, until they color and start to caramelize, 10 to 12 minutes.

Bread Pudding Soufflé with Whiskey Sauce

For this you need three elements: bread pudding, meringue, and sauce. The first and last may be made in advance. You can freeze leftover bread pudding for another batch of soufflés or you can serve it as is, with the Whiskey Sauce.

Bread Pudding

1 cup sugar
¾ teaspoon cinnamon
Pinch of nutmeg
1 whole egg plus 1 egg white, lightly beaten
1 cup half-and-half
1 teaspoon vanilla extract
4 to 5 cups cubed New Orleans French Bread (page 27)
¼ cup raisins

Whiskey Sauce

1½ teaspoons cornstarch
1 tablespoon water
½ cup heavy cream
2 tablespoons sugar
2 tablespoons bourbon

Meringue

8 egg whites
½ cup sugar

Make the bread pudding: Preheat the oven to 350 degrees. Grease an 8 x 8-inch pan.

Mix the sugar, cinnamon, and nutmeg in a large bowl. Beat in the egg and egg white, then stir in the half-and-half and vanilla. Add bread and raisins and stir. Pour into prepared pan and bake until lightly browned and a toothpick comes out clean, about 45 minutes. Cool.

Make the sauce: Whisk together the cornstarch and water. In a small saucepan over medium heat, bring cream to a boil. Add cornstarch mixture, whisking vigorously. Let mixture boil. Then remove from heat and stir in sugar and bourbon. Allow to cool, then refrigerate.

Make the meringue: Preheat oven to 350 degrees. Butter 6 individual ½-cup custard cups.

In a large bowl, whip the egg whites until foamy. Continue to whip, adding sugar gradually, until shiny and thick.

In a large bowl, break half the bread pudding — reserve the rest for another use — into small bits (use your hands or a large spoon) and gently stir in half the meringue. Then fold in half of the remaining meringue, reserving the rest. Spoon the mixture into the prepared cups and top each with a swirl of the reserved meringue. Bake in a water bath until tops are golden, about 20 minutes.

To serve, warm the Whiskey Sauce in a double boiler. Poke down the tops of the soufflés and spoon in a bit of the sauce.

Serves 6

Opposite: *French windows facing St. Charles Avenue.*
Above: *Garden statue.* **Right:** *Bread Pudding Soufflé with Whiskey Sauce.*

This glamorous dinner combines a bit of both old and new New Orleans food. Shrimp remoulade, which starts the meal, is certainly an enduring favorite. I can't imagine you not having tried it at some point, but if you haven't, it's time to rectify that lapse. This recipe is about as good as it gets — which is pretty good indeed. The main course is

FORMAL DINNER FOR FRIENDS

Grinnan-Reily House

Shrimp Remoulade

Braised Pheasant with Champagne Sauce

White Pepper Carrots

Stuffed Cabbage Rolls

Greens and Mushroom Salad

Fig Tart

Creole Cream Cheese Ice Cream

Schramsberg Blanc de Noir, Napa 1985

braised pheasant. Although southerners in general are particularly fond of game, pheasant is not native to the Deep South, so it is a comparative newcomer to local cooking. I've heard people complain about pheasant not being moist enough. Maybe sometime, but not this version! Here it is served with a Champagne sauce and accompanied by white pepper carrots and cabbage rolls that are so good they could probably become a little supper by themselves. The salad is peppery greens tossed with assorted fresh mushrooms, a perfect transition to dessert, a luscious tart made with that great southern delight, fig preserves, as a filling. And as if that weren't enough, there's Creole cream cheese ice cream to top it with. Take it from me, this ice cream is in a class by itself.

Opposite: *Braised Pheasant with Champagne Sauce, Stuffed Cabbage Rolls, and White Pepper Carrots.*

Shrimp Remoulade

An evergreen favorite revisited.

1 large celery rib, chopped coarse
2 large green onions, chopped coarse, with some green
½ cup coarsely chopped parsley
⅛ lemon (1 wedge)
3 eggs
¼ cup prepared horseradish
¼ cup Creole mustard (see Note, page 87)
¼ cup yellow mustard
½ cup catsup
1½ teaspoons salt, or to taste
2 teaspoons paprika
¼ cup Worcestershire Sauce, preferably homemade
  (page 140)
1½ cups vegetable oil
¼ cup white wine vinegar
About 2 cups shredded lettuce
36 shrimp, peeled, deveined, and boiled
6 lemon wedges
12 toast points

Puree celery, green onions, parsley, and lemon wedge together in a food processor. Scrape out into a bowl and mix in eggs, horseradish, mustards, catsup, salt, paprika, and Worcestershire. Drizzle in oil, whisking. Stir in the vinegar. Correct seasoning if needed.

  To assemble, place a bed of shredded lettuce on 6 individual small plates or in small bowls. Divide shrimp among them and top with sauce. Serve with a lemon wedge and slices of thin toasted bread. Pass the extra sauce.

Serves 6

Right: *Greek Revival portico.*

Braised Pheasant with Champagne Sauce

3 whole pheasant breasts, halved and boned with
    wing bone left in (see Note)
1 teaspoon Creole Seasoning (page 109)
¼ cup clarified unsalted butter
¼ cup reduced Pheasant Stock (recipe follows)
2 cups chicken stock

Champagne Sauce
1 tablespoon unsalted butter, plus ¼ cup cut in bits
1½ teaspoons minced garlic
2 tablespoons minced shallots
2 cups Champagne
2 tablespoons sugar
1 tablespoon cornstarch
1 tablespoon water
½ cup half-and-half

Preheat oven to 350 degrees.

Rub pheasant breasts with the Creole Seasoning. In
a skillet, heat clarified butter to very hot over high
flame. Brown breasts, about 2 minutes per side.
Transfer to an ovenproof pan skin side up. Pour in
the reduced Pheasant Stock and enough chicken
stock so that the bottoms of the breasts are
submerged but the skin is exposed. Bake for about
20 minutes, until tender. Remove to a platter and
keep warm. Reserve pan juices.

Make the sauce: Melt 1 tablespoon butter in a deep
skillet over medium heat, then add the garlic and
shallots. Cover, lower heat, and allow the vegetables
to sweat for 2 to 3 minutes. Add Champagne and
cook, uncovered, over medium-high heat for 6 to 8
minutes. About 4 minutes into this cooking time,
stir in sugar. Dissolve the cornstarch in the
tablespoon of water and add this, stirring. The sauce
will begin to darken and turn syrupy. At the end of
the reduction stir in the reserved pan juices and the
half-and-half; heat through. Off the heat, whisk in
the cold butter. Correct seasoning.

Serve warm breast with sauce spooned over it.

Serves 6

**Note: Reserve the rest of the pheasant meat for the Stuffed
Cabbage Rolls (page 132) and the bones for the stock.**

Pheasant Stock

2 tablespoons unsalted butter
2 pheasant carcasses
2 cups very coarsely chopped celery
1½ cups very coarsely chopped carrot
2 cups very coarsely chopped onion
2 large bay leaves

Preheat oven to 400 degrees.

Grease a roasting pan with the butter and chop up
the carcasses into large pieces. Roast, turning pieces
after about 15 minutes. After about 30 minutes add
vegetables and continue to roast, turning
occasionally, for another 45 minutes. Dump this
mixture into a pot and cover with cold water. Add
bay leaves. Deglaze the roasting pan with a little
water when it heats and return it to the pot.

Bring to a boil, then reduce to a simmer. Cook for
1 to 1½ hours. Strain bones and solids out of stock
and discard. Cool and refrigerate stock. Skim off
congealed fat and discard.

To use stock, reduce it by bringing it to a very slow
boil and cooking it down to about ¼ cup. By then it
will be dark and syrupy.

White Pepper Carrots
*We used baby carrots for the photograph, but I've
substituted carrot rings here.*

2 tablespoons unsalted butter
2 tablespoons sugar
1 to 2 teaspoons salt, to taste
1 teaspoon white pepper
2½ to 3 cups carrot rings, steamed tender,
    about 5 minutes
1 tablespoon minced parsley

Melt butter in a large skillet over medium heat. Stir
in sugar, salt, and pepper. Add carrots, tossing
lightly. Heat through. Toss with the parsley.

Serves 6

ABOUT THE HOUSE

I think you can tell when a house is loved by those who live in it. I don't mean loved as a symbol of accomplishment, but loved as a place to be at home. This is such a house. I've got to admit to a special weakness for it, and not simply because it is so beautifully designed and furnished. I've known the place for forty years and have seen it occupied by two generations of the same family, each of which has imbued it with their own taste and style.

Grinnan-Reily House was built in 1850 for Robert A. Grinnan, an Englishman newly arrived in New Orleans. Here is a far-from-usual case: We have all the facts of the house's beginnings, including a contract between Grinnan and the builder, John Sewell, dated 10 April 1850. Among other things, the contract tells us that Grinnan knew how to strike a bargain, for not only are the details of the house meticulously spelled out, but so too is a completion date — with penalties for noncompliance. The price was $19,500, a pretty tidy sum in antebellum times; the designer was the famed Irish-American architect Henry Howard.

Left: *Grinnan-Reily House.* **Above:** *Detail of Corinthian column in the front hall.*
Below: *Looking out at the entrance garden.*

The contract clearly specifies that glass throughout was to be French cylinder glass; the exterior was to be painted with four coats of "good English white lead in oil"; the doors were to be of Santo Domingo mahogany; the hardware to be silver-plated. Among the out-of-the-ordinary items were two water closets (again of Santo Domingo mahogany) and two lead-lined bathtubs; most unusual of all was the city's first "rainbath" — or shower.

Over the years, outbuildings were added and removed, and the slave quarters were ultimately connected to the main house. When first built, the house was slightly hemmed in on its plot, but as time passed more property was purchased to create the side garden.

The house was completely renovated several years ago, making it if anything more beautiful than ever and ensuring that it will survive for others to love and be sheltered by.

Opposite: *Reflection of the drawing room.* **Left:** *Looking out into the side garden.* **Above:** *Drawing room mirror.* **Below:** *Curved entrance stair.*

Stuffed Cabbage Rolls

You could also probably make these with duck legs.

1 small head of green cabbage

Filling

Reserved meat from Braised Pheasant (page 127),
   including livers, gizzards, and hearts
3 tablespoons clarified unsalted butter
1 medium white onion, minced
¼ cup minced garlic
1 teaspoon salt
1 teaspoon white pepper
Pinch of cayenne
1 cup cooked rice

Sauce

1 tablespoon vegetable oil
2 celery ribs, chopped
2 medium green bell peppers, chopped
2 medium onions, chopped
1 bay leaf
¼ cup chopped garlic
5 medium tomatoes, peeled, seeded, and chopped
   coarse (see Note)
2 teaspoons salt
1½ teaspoons white pepper
¼ teaspoon cayenne
1 generous tablespoon minced fresh basil, oregano,
   or tarragon, or a mixture of all three (see Note)

Peel off and discard loose outer leaves of the
cabbage. Remove part of the core by cutting a 1-inch
cone-shaped piece from the base. Place cabbage, base
end down, in 2 inches of boiling water and cover.
This makes the leaves easier to separate. Remove
leaves as they can be peeled off, setting them aside.
Continue until all leaves are separated. Grind or
chop the pheasant coarsely.

Make the filling: Heat the butter over a high flame in
a large skillet. When very hot add onion and garlic
and sauté 2 minutes. Add chopped meat and
continue to cook, stirring, until meat starts to turn
brown, 4 to 5 minutes. Stir in seasoning and then
rice, mixing well but lightly.

Make the sauce: Heat oil in a large heavy skillet over
medium flame. Sauté celery, peppers, and onions
until wilted and onions begin to caramelize, 8 to 10
minutes, stirring frequently. Stir in bay leaf and garlic.
Continue to cook for another minute or two. Add
tomatoes, salt, pepper, and cayenne. Simmer over low
heat for another 15 to 20 minutes. After cooking
about 10 minutes, stir in herbs. Correct seasoning.

Preheat oven to 300 degrees.

Cut part of the rib on each cabbage leaf and lay
them flat. Place about 2½ tablespoons of the filling
in the center of each, tuck in the sides, and roll into
a small packet. Place them in a 10 x 12-inch
ovenproof pan as you go, continuing until all the
filling is used. Cover with the tomato sauce and bake
for 20 to 25 minutes.

Makes 6 servings

Note: You may use a 28-ounce can of peeled tomatoes (no
paste), drained and chopped, in place of fresh. And you may
substitute half the amount of fresh in dry herbs. If you do,
however, add them at the beginning, when you sauté the
vegetables.

Opposite: *Mantel detail.* Left: *Hall credenza with Blanc de Chine cocks.* Below: *Family-initialed Chinese export tea service.*

Above: Greens and Mushroom Salad. *Below:* Fig Tart with Creole Cream Cheese Ice Cream.

Greens and Mushroom Salad

Use any kind or combination of fresh mushrooms you like in this salad.

⅓ cup white wine vinegar
1 cup olive oil
1 teaspoon salt, or to taste
¼ teaspoon white pepper, or to taste
1 tablespoon minced shallots
1 tablespoon minced garlic
1 tablespoon each diced roasted, peeled, and seeded red, yellow, and green pepper (or the total in red pepper)
3 cups mixed greens, cleaned and torn into bite-size bits
1 cup sliced mushrooms

Whisk together the vinegar, oil, salt, and pepper. Stir in shallots, garlic, and peppers.

Toss greens and mushrooms together. Spoon enough vinaigrette over all to coat. Toss.

Serves 6

Fig Tart

This may be made with fig preserves or fig jam. The taste of the finished tart reminds me of a Fig Newton.

¾ cup sugar
⅔ cup pecans
1 cup (2 sticks) unsalted butter, softened
3 eggs
¼ teaspoon vanilla extract
2¼ cups flour
½ teaspoon cinnamon
1 teaspoon baking powder
¼ cup milk
2½ cups fig preserves, with juice

Grind sugar and pecans together in a food processor until very fine. There should be no recognizable pieces. Cream butter with the sugar-pecan mixture until light and fluffy. Add 2 of the eggs and the vanilla. Beat until smooth. Sift flour, cinnamon, and baking powder together. Add to the egg mixture, beating just until dough comes together; do not overmix. Divide in two. Press into two 9-inch disks between sheets of waxed paper. Refrigerate for at least an hour.

Preheat oven to 350 degrees and line the bottom of a 9-inch cake pan with parchment.

Roll out one piece of the dough into a circle about ¼ inch thick. Line bottom of the pan. (You may use the bottom of the pan to mark the circle so you can get a perfect fit.) If dough tears, press it back together.

Beat the remaining egg with milk.

Take half of the other piece of dough and roll it into a ¾-inch rope about equal to the circumference of the pan. (You may do this in 2 pieces.) Run the rope around the inside of the pan and press it into place. It should line the sides and come up to the top of the pan. Crimp. Paint all with the egg wash. Pour in fig preserves. This filling should come just to the top of the pan.

Roll out the remaining dough, including any scraps from the "rope," to about ¼-inch thickness. Cut into ¾-inch strips. Place strips on top of filling to make a lattice, pressing down lightly to seal where strips cross one another and touch the sides. Brush with remaining egg wash. Bake until golden, about 45 minutes.

Serve with vanilla ice cream or Creole Cream Cheese Ice Cream.

Serves 8

Creole Cream Cheese Ice Cream

This makes an ultra creamy ice cream.

1 cup sugar
3¼ cups half-and-half
4 egg yolks, lightly beaten
¾ cup sour cream
½ cup Creole cream cheese (or sour cream)

Place sugar, half-and-half, and egg yolks into a heavy saucepan and mix well. Cook over moderate heat, stirring constantly, until mixture coats the back of a spoon, 8 to 10 minutes; do not boil. Remove from heat and strain into a bowl set into another bowl of cracked ice. Stir to cool. Whisk in sour cream and cream cheese. Freeze in an ice cream maker according to manufacturer's instructions.

Makes about 1 quart

A SMALL DINNER PARTY

McDermott-Smith House

Crawfish-Stuffed Eggplant "Tortillas"
with Tomatillo Sauce

Panned Rabbit with Homemade
Worcestershire Sauce and Roasted Garlic

Sweet Potatoes Brabant

New Orleans Coleslaw

Creole Cheesecake with Caramel Sauce

DeLoach "Russian River Valley"
Zinfandel, Sonoma 1989

There's lots of interesting stuff in this menu. To begin there's a strictly southern take on stuffed tortillas: thin slices of eggplant stuffed with crawfish and other good things served on a pool of tomatillo sauce. They are so good I bet you'll build a little lunch around them sometime. Following this southern fried-southwest beginning is mustard-rubbed panned rabbit, a type of meat that is just beginning to gain favor in these parts. The rabbit is accented by homemade Worcestershire Sauce; this is much more subtle than the commercial variety and something you'll find plenty of uses for. Accompaniments are sweet potatoes brabant, a nice variation of an old reliable, and coleslaw made the way they like it down here. Dessert is cheesecake prepared with the local cream cheese, which gives the cake its own special flavor. The cheesecake is topped with chocolate and accompanied by caramel sauce. However, the cake is also great unadorned.

Above: *Panned Rabbit with Homemade Worcestershire Sauce and Roasted Garlic, Sweet Potatoes Brabant, and New Orleans Coleslaw.* **Opposite:** *Shuttered entrance door.*

Crawfish-Stuffed Eggplant "Tortillas" with Tomatillo Sauce

Although it wouldn't be the same, because crawfish have such a different flavor, you could substitute shrimp here. Now don't be daunted by the length of this recipe. There are simply a number of quick and simple steps to explain. Start off by reading this through so you'll know what you're doing, then begin by making the sauces and accompaniments.

Tomatillo Sauce

1 pound tomatillos, husks removed
¼ medium onion, chopped
2 teaspoons minced garlic
1 teaspoon minced jalapeño pepper
1 tablespoon vegetable oil
½ cup water
½ teaspoon salt
¼ teaspoon sugar

Salsa

2 cups finely diced ripe tomatoes
3 tablespoons diced red bell pepper
3 tablespoons diced green bell pepper
3 tablespoons minced white onion
2 teaspoons minced jalapeño pepper
1 generous tablespoon minced cilantro
1 teaspoon salt
½ teaspoon white pepper

"Tortillas"

6 ⅛-inch thick slices of eggplant (cut from the center of a large eggplant)
1 cup toasted bread crumbs
2½ teaspoons Creole Seasoning (page 109)
1 cup flour
2 eggs
½ cup milk
½ cup vegetable oil

Filling

1 tablespoon vegetable oil
3 tablespoons diced red bell pepper
3 tablespoons diced green bell pepper
2 teaspoons minced garlic
3 tablespoons minced white onion
¾ pound peeled crawfish tails
1 teaspoon Creole Seasoning
2 teaspoons Tabasco sauce

2 teaspoons Worcestershire sauce
6 ounces jalapeño cheese, shredded
2 tablespoons finely chopped green onion tops

Garnish

½ cup sour cream
½ cup snipped chives

Make the sauce: Puree the tomatillos, onion, garlic, and jalapeño in a food processor.

Heat the oil in a nonreactive skillet over medium heat. Add the puree and bring to a boil. Reduce heat and simmer for 10 minutes. Add water, salt, and sugar and cook for another 12 to 15 minutes. Reserve.

Make the salsa: Mix all the ingredients together and let marinate for at least an hour before serving. You can refrigerate this, but allow it to come back to room temperature.

Make the "tortillas": Pat the eggplant slices dry. Mix the flour with 2 teaspoons of Creole Seasoning and spread out on a piece of waxed paper. In a flat bowl, whisk the eggs and milk. Sprinkle the eggplant with ½ teaspoon Creole Seasoning. Dip the slices first in the flour, then into the egg wash, and then into the bread crumbs. Set aside on a tray.

Heat the oil to almost smoking in a large skillet over high heat. Fry the eggplant quickly until golden on both sides. Set aside to drain on paper towels.

Make the filling: Heat a skillet over high heat. Add the oil, peppers, garlic, and onions and sauté for a minute or so. Add the crawfish, Creole Seasoning, Tabasco, and Worcestershire and continue to sauté, stirring, for another 3 or 4 minutes. Remove from heat and stir in the cheese and green onion.

Preheat the oven to 350 degrees.

Oil a small pan just large enough to hold the stuffed tortillas. Spread about 2 tablespoons of the filling over half of an eggplant slice; fold the slice over carefully and transfer it to the prepared pan. Repeat. (You can cover this dish with a damp cloth and hold it for about an hour.) Bake until heated through, 5 to 10 minutes.

To serve: Mix the sour cream and chives. Heat the Tomatillo Sauce. Spread a slick of sauce on individual plates and top with a tortilla. Garnish with the salsa and the sour cream.

Serves 6

Above: *Crawfish-Stuffed Eggplant "Tortillas" with Tomatillo Sauce.* **Below:** *Trompe l'oeil in the entrance hall.*

Panned Rabbit with Homemade Worcestershire Sauce and Roasted Garlic

Except for the Homemade Worcestershire Sauce — which you would have made in advance and had on hand — this is about as simple an entrée as you could come up with.

2 3-pound rabbits, boned and cut into serving-size pieces
2 to 3 tablespoons Creole mustard (see Note, page 87)
2 teaspoons salt
3 teaspoons white pepper
4 to 6 tablespoons clarified butter
Homemade Worcestershire Sauce (recipe follows)
Roasted Garlic (recipe follows)

Lightly pound rabbit pieces between sheets of waxed paper to flatten slightly. Rub each piece of rabbit with about ½ teaspoon of the mustard. Combine salt and pepper and season the rabbit on all sides.

Place butter (start with the 4 tablespoons and add more if needed) in a large skillet and heat on a high flame. Sauté rabbit pieces until golden, turning once or twice, about 2½ minutes.

Serve topped with Homemade Worcestershire Sauce and half a head of Roasted Garlic.

Serves 6

Opposite: *The McDermott-Smith house at left. Grandfather clock at right.*

Homemade Worcestershire Sauce

1 tablespoon olive oil
6 ounces peeled fresh horseradish, chopped (weight after peeling), about 1 cup
2 medium white onions, chopped
3 tablespoons minced jalapeño pepper
3 tablespoons minced garlic
1 teaspoon coarsely ground black pepper
2 cups water
4 cups distilled white vinegar
1 cup molasses
2 cups dark corn syrup
1 ounce chopped anchovy fillets, drained (½ flat can)
12 whole cloves
1 tablespoon salt
1 lemon, peeled, pith removed, and chopped (discard rind and pith)

In a medium saucepan, heat oil over medium heat and add horseradish, onions, pepper, and garlic. Sauté until translucent, 5 to 8 minutes. Add all the other ingredients and bring to a boil. Turn heat down and simmer for 1 hour. Strain through a double thickness of cheesecloth and store in a wooden cask if possible. This is best if allowed to mature for about a month before using.

Makes approximately 3 pints

Roasted Garlic

People who love it smear roasted garlic on French bread to eat along with the rabbit.

3 large garlic heads, cut in two crossways
3 tablespoons olive oil
Salt

Preheat oven to 400 degrees.

Place garlic halves, cut side up, in a small pan and drizzle ½ tablespoon of the olive oil over each half head, then sprinkle with salt. Bake until softened and turning golden, about 20 minutes or so.

Accompany each serving of rabbit with a half head of garlic.

ABOUT THE HOUSE

In early 1882 a permit was issued to Thomas McDermott for a $12,500 house. In May of that year a notice appeared in *The Daily Picayune* reporting that the "fine two-story dwelling was nearing completion" and the following year McDermott was listed as living in his new house in the city directory. After that McDermott apparently settled down to live a quiet life. We do know that McDermott shared the house with two maiden sisters who had the habit of tying paper flowers to the hedges when the hedges didn't produce any flowers of their own. That this piece of inconsequential trivia is all that remained in the memory of their neighbors tells us how unruffled and contented the trio's existence was.

Apparently McDermott had a desire for comfort and an understanding of some simple ways to ensure that his house would provide him with the cool breezes so treasured by early residents of this city. Almost one foot of insulating air space was part of the walls, so when the inside blinds on all the windows were closed against the midday heat a pleasant and fairly even interior climate was possible year-round. This, taken with almost every room opening onto some sort of gallery or balcony where one could sit in secluded comfort after sundown to enjoy whatever river breeze might blow, tells you that McDermott knew his city and how to be at ease in it.

By and large, the numerous owners must have been satisfied with the way this hybrid Italianate—modern French house looked. It's a compliment to McDermott's taste (an attribute he probably wouldn't have prized had he been told of it) that he and his flower-tying sisters would still easily recognize their gentle home today.

Sweet Potatoes Brabant

*These are delicious, but they do take a bit
of doing. If you want sweet potatoes but don't want
the work, just bake 'em or try the Sweet
Potato Cakes on page 171.*

3 medium sweet potatoes, about 2½ pounds, peeled
    and cut into 1-inch dice
Vegetable oil for deep-frying
¼ cup clarified butter (or olive oil)
2 tablespoons minced garlic
½ teaspoon salt
2 tablespoons minced parsley

Put sweet potatoes in a large pot of well-salted water
and bring to a boil over medium heat. Cook 30
minutes. Drain and chill for at least 30 minutes.

Heat vegetable oil in a deep-fat fryer to 350
degrees and fry potatoes until they are golden, 2 to
2½ minutes. Drain on paper towels.

Heat butter in a large skillet over high heat. Add
garlic and salt. Continue to cook, shaking pan, until
garlic just begins to brown, about 1 minute. Add
potatoes and shake pan to coat them with butter,
stir in parsley, and serve immediately.

Serves 6

Above: *Armoire with bombé base.* **Above right:** *Creole Cheesecake
with Caramel Sauce.* **Right:** *Fortuny curtain near a Japanese
secretary.*

New Orleans Coleslaw

This is a typically pungent mix.

4 cups shredded green cabbage
½ cup shredded peeled carrot
6 tablespoons mayonnaise
2½ tablespoons Creole mustard (see Note, page 87)
1¼ tablespoons white wine vinegar
½ teaspoon salt
½ teaspoon white pepper
½ teaspoon sugar
1½ teaspoons minced parsley
1 tablespoon fresh lemon juice

Toss cabbage and carrot together in a large bowl. Beat together all other ingredients and pour onto vegetables. Toss to coat well.

Serves 6

Creole Cheesecake with Caramel Sauce

Don't make your servings of this too large — it's rich. Besides, your guests can always come back for seconds. Be sure to ask them.

Crust
¾ pound graham crackers
¾ cup sugar
¾ cup (1½ sticks) unsalted butter, melted

Filling
1½ pounds cream cheese
¾ cup sugar
1 whole egg plus 1 egg white
1 cup plus 2 tablespoons Creole cream cheese (or sour cream)

Topping
1 cup sour cream
3 tablespoons sugar
Shaved bittersweet and white chocolate

Caramel Sauce (recipe follows)

Preheat oven to 250 degrees.
  Make the crust: Pulverize the graham crackers in a food processor. Add sugar and pulse for a second or two. Add butter and pulse to combine. Put about half the mixture into a 9-inch springform pan. Press along the sides to make a thick crust. Add the rest and press it onto the bottom of the pan.
  Make the filling: Blend the cream cheese and sugar in a food processor until just smooth. Beat together the eggs and Creole cream cheese. Combine the 2 mixtures and blend well. Scrape into the prepared pan and bake for 10 minutes. Reduce heat to 225 degrees and cook for 1 hour and 50 minutes.
  Make the topping: Whisk together the sour cream and sugar. Spread it over the cheesecake as soon as you take it out of the oven. Start spreading at the center so you don't pull crumbs into the topping.
  Allow the cake to cool, then refrigerate at least 2 hours before serving. Sprinkle with shaved chocolate. Cut with a knife dipped into very hot water then dried. Serve with Caramel Sauce.

Serves 8 to 12

Caramel Sauce

2 cups sugar
¼ cup light corn syrup
¼ cup water
2 cups chilled heavy cream

Place sugar, corn syrup, and water in a medium saucepan and bring to a boil over high heat. Boil until medium golden, about 10 minutes. Remove from heat and carefully add cream, stirring. This will bubble up a lot — which is why you should use a medium or large saucepan. Return to heat and bring back to a boil, stirring. Reduce heat to medium-low and continue to boil lightly to reduce and thicken, about 8 to 10 minutes. Cool and correct consistency with a little more cream if necessary. It should be thick but pourable.

Makes about 2 cups

ROAST PORK FOR A PARTY

Montgomery-Hero-Reynoir House

Roast Rack of Pork with Port Sauce

Turnips and Beets

Sautéed Bananas

Peppered Onion Relish

Pound Cake with Strawberries and Cream

Chateau Ste. Michelle Merlot,
Washington State 1988

is a wonderfully seductive streak of "retro" right under the surface to be found even in the most innovative local cooking and preferences. One proof is that there are still quite a large number of restaurants here that serve today almost exactly the same basic dishes they opened with fifty to seventy-five years ago. ∾ So here is a party meal of the sort that I think would still have strong appeal for most people hereabouts. It doesn't include fish or seafood as so many menus in this book do; it's built around that other great southern plantation staple — pork! Accompaniments are root vegetables, beets and turnips, and peppered onion relish. We've also included sautéed bananas. ∾ Dessert is old-fashioned pound cake with strawberries and whipped cream. Who could ask for anything more?

Left: *The meal on the sideboard.* **Opposite:** *Afternoon in the living room.*

ABOUT THE HOUSE

During the golden era of construction in the Garden District, Henry Howard and the Galliers, father and son, were the reigning architects. Both Howard and Gallier, Jr., have been credited with designing this house for Archibald Montgomery, with Gallier, Jr., ahead in the race. There is also a great deal of romantic hyperbole about the house being designed as a tribute to the remarkable beauty and charm of Mrs. Montgomery, who is reputed to have been quite a belle in her day.

Whatever its inspiration, the house is spectacular. The actual date of its completion has been set variously as before and after the Civil War, but Gallier's (or Howard's) combination of styles in the structure argues for the later date. Things were changing rapidly in the mid 1860s, including adherence to strict design principles. The house is so eclectic that it almost defies

categorization; it has variously been referred to as Gothic or Italianate with classic overtones. In the final analysis these liberties account for the immense charm of the place.

The interior arrangement was conventional enough, with six rooms downstairs with fourteen-foot ceilings and six above with thirteen-foot ceilings. However, when it came to ornamentation, tradition was left in the dust. Italianate rosettes, mantels, windows, and doors lend the rooms a light and airy feeling. To enhance the light feeling of the interiors, especially on the left side of the house, double-hung casement windows with arched tops run from floor to ceiling.

The exterior is an artful blending of elliptical arches, slender columns, massive balustrades, and Gothic-like moldings. Miraculously, it creates a harmonious whole — whatever its inspiration.

Roast Rack of Pork with Port Sauce

Now who doesn't like a good pork roast? Here it is, in all its succulent goodness!

1 12-pound center cut loin of pork (weight with bones)
1½ teaspoons salt
1½ teaspoons black pepper
1 tablespoon minced rosemary leaves, or 1½ teaspoons dried
3 tablespoons minced garlic
½ cup olive oil
½ cup port wine
2 cups unsalted beef or veal stock

Preheat oven to 375 degrees.

Have your butcher remove the chine and feather bones and clean the rib bones back to the "eye."

Mix together the salt, pepper, and rosemary and rub all over meat. Then rub and pat garlic over all, and if you can, force some garlic between the roast and rib bones. (Try making incisions with the point of a knife.) Heat oil in a large skillet over a high flame and sear meat on all sides until it is well browned, 10 minutes or more.

Place on a rack in a roasting pan and cook for 1 hour, or until a meat thermometer registers 160 to 165 degrees.

Remove meat to a warm serving platter and cover lightly with foil. Allow to rest 15 minutes before removing bones and carving.

Meanwhile, make the sauce. Pour all fat from the roasting pan, then, over high heat on top of the stove, deglaze pan with the port, stirring and scraping up the browned bits so they will dissolve. Add stock and boil slowly for about 15 minutes until sauce reduces and thickens slightly. Skim off any surface fat and serve with the pork.

Serves 8

Opposite: *Montgomery-Hero-Reynoir House.* **Left:** *Detail of the gallery.*

Turnips and Beets

The method of cooking and preparation for both of these is the same, but they should be cooked separately to keep the turnips from being colored by the beets.

6 medium turnips, peeled and quartered
2 tablespoons unsalted butter
Salt and white pepper to taste
4 tablespoons minced parsley
6 medium beets, peeled and quartered

Place turnips in a saucepan and cover with well-salted water. Bring to a boil over high heat, then turn heat down to a light boil and cook until just fork-tender, about 15 minutes. If not using right away, plunge in cold water and drain.

To serve, melt 1 tablespoon butter in a large skillet and sauté turnips until warmed through, about 2 minutes. Toss with salt, pepper, and 2 tablespoons of the parsley.

To prepare beets, use the same method as above.

Serves 8

Sautéed Bananas

This is done rather quickly so wait until the last minute.

4 tablespoons (½ stick) unsalted butter
1 packed tablespoon dark brown sugar
Pinch of salt
Pinch of white pepper
8 medium bananas, peeled and sliced diagonally into
    1-inch pieces

Place all ingredients except bananas in a large skillet and heat over high heat. When bubbly, add bananas and cook, tossing lightly, just long enough to coat and heat through, 1 to 2 minutes. Serve hot.

Serves 8

Peppered Onion Relish

Shallots could be added to this mixture.

2 tablespoons unsalted butter
4 cups diced onions
1 teaspoon salt
1 tablespoon sugar
½ teaspoon black pepper
2 tablespoons white pepper

Heat butter over a high flame until it begins to brown; add onions. Continue to cook over fairly high heat, tossing, until onions are browned but not burned, about 3 to 4 minutes. Add other ingredients and cook for another minute. Check seasoning.

Makes about 3 cups

Above: *Far end of the living room.* **Opposite:** *Pound Cake with Strawberries and Cream.*

Pound Cake with Strawberries and Cream

Of course, this simple dessert could be varied by serving other types of fresh fruit with it.

1⅓ cups unsalted butter, softened
1⅓ cups sugar
2 cups unsifted flour
1 teaspoon baking powder
½ teaspoon salt
5 large eggs
¼ cup milk
1 teaspoon vanilla extract
Strawberries and Cream (recipe follows)

Preheat oven to 350 degrees. Butter and flour a 5¼ x 9-inch loaf pan.

Cream butter and sugar together until light and fluffy. Sift together the flour, baking powder, and salt. In a separate bowl, beat together the eggs, milk, and vanilla. Add the flour mixture to the butter mixture in 3 batches, alternating with the milk mixture and ending with the flour. Do not overmix.

Batter will be stiff.

Scrape into pan and smooth the top.

Bake for about 1 hour, until a cake tester comes out clean. Allow to cool slightly, run a knife around the sides, and invert onto a rack.

Slice and serve topped with Strawberries and Cream.

Serves 10 or more

Strawberries and Cream

2 cups strawberries, stemmed and halved
3 tablespoons sugar
1 cup heavy cream
½ teaspoon vanilla extract

Place strawberries in a bowl and sprinkle with 2 tablespoons of the sugar. Cover and refrigerate for an hour or so. Whip cream to soft peaks and stir in the remaining tablespoon of sugar and the vanilla.

Serve with the pound cake.

Roses in New Orleans tend to be rather temperamental because of the bugs and mildew the warm, humid climate encourages. Regardless, roses seem part of every garden. The ones at Payne-Strachan House are particularly lovely and there is even a beautiful little tea house to one side of where they are planted in a formal setting. This serene

LUNCH OVERLOOKING THE GARDEN

Payne-Strachan House

Warm Yellow Fin Tuna Salad

Smoked Chicken Salad

Focaccia Rounds

Sun-Dried Tomato Toasts

Lora Brody Chocolate Cake

Hess Select 1989 Chardonnay

spot inspired us to come up with a simple lunch that could be easily transported out to be eaten while gazing at the flowers. ∾ Actually, we devised two lunches, so you can have a choice of either fish or chicken. The first is a salad composed of warm yellow fin tuna resting on a bed of angel hair pasta tossed with pimiento and green onions and placed on an assortment of greens. We could have stopped there, but there's broccoli, cucumber, and tomatoes for garnish. ∾ The other lunch is also a salad, built around smoked chicken, which can often be purchased ready to serve at specialty markets. It's garnished with all sorts of interesting things. To add to the mix are sun-dried tomato toast, focaccia rounds, and chutney. ∾ Dessert for both lunches is a flourless chocolate cake with a dark chocolate glaze and white chocolate sauce. Guaranteed to make chocolate freaks crazy.

Left: *The tea house.* Opposite: *Ceres surrounded by yew.*

Above: *Warm Yellow Fin Tuna Salad.* **Below left:** *A pair of eighteenth-century chairs.* **Below right:** *Smoked Chicken Salad and Focaccia Rounds.*

Warm Yellow Fin Tuna Salad
You may use as many of the garnishes here as you have time for or want.

1 pound angel hair pasta
¼ cup vegetable oil
¼ cup plus 1 teaspoon rice wine vinegar
½ cup drained canned chopped pimiento
Green end of 6 green onions, chopped
¾ teaspoon salt
¼ teaspoon white pepper
12 small broccoli florets
1 medium cucumber, peeled, seeded, and cut into
  2 x ¼-inch strips
1 teaspoon toasted sesame seeds

Wasabi Dressing
2 tablespoons wasabi
¼ cup water
1 egg yolk
2 cups vegetable oil
¼ cup rice wine vinegar
¼ teaspoon salt
⅛ teaspoon white pepper

Assembly
1 pound yellow fin tuna cut into ½-inch thick
  medallions
¼ cup soy sauce
3 medium ripe tomatoes, cut into wedges
6 Bibb lettuce leaves
6 radicchio leaves

Cook pasta in salted water according to package directions. Rinse in cold water and drain. Toss with the oil, ¼ cup of the vinegar, pimiento, green onion tops, ½ teaspoon of the salt, and white pepper. Set aside. Blanch broccoli florets in boiling salted water for 1 minute and immediately immerse in cold water. Drain and set aside. Toss cucumber with the remaining teaspoon of vinegar and ¼ teaspoon of salt. Sprinkle with sesame seeds, toss, and set aside.

Make the dressing: Blend wasabi and water. Set aside for 15 minutes. Whisk egg yolk and add oil in a thin steady stream, whisking until all the oil is incorporated and mixture is the texture of mayonnaise. Stir in vinegar, salt, and pepper. Mix in wasabi.

Assemble the salad: Preheat broiler and rub medallions with the soy sauce. Allow to rest for 5 minutes. Meanwhile, arrange pasta, lettuces, tomatoes, cucumbers, and broccoli as you wish on individual plates.

Put tuna on a baking sheet and broil for 1 minute on each side. Immediately place equal portions of tuna on each serving of pasta. Drizzle Wasabi Dressing over top. Serve extra on the side.

Serves 6

Smoked Chicken Salad
This is a fairly generous amount of chicken, so you may want to reduce the quantity.

3 small (2½- to 3-pound) smoked chickens at room
  temperature, split
1 head *frisée* lettuce, washed, dried, and torn into pieces
Rice Wine Vinaigrette (recipe follows)
24 to 36 Kalamata olives
1 pound red seedless grapes
¾ pound ricotta cheese, cut into 12 wedges
1 cup Pear and Chili Chutney (page 155)

Warm chicken in a 325-degree oven for 3 to 4 minutes. Meanwhile, toss *frisée* lettuce with enough Rice Wine Vinaigrette to coat leaves lightly. Divide among 6 plates and top with the olives. Place half a chicken on each plate. Accompany by bunches of grapes, cheese wedges, and a dollop of the chutney.

Serves 6

Rice Wine Vinaigrette
⅓ cup rice wine vinegar
¾ cup vegetable oil
¼ cup olive oil
½ teaspoon salt
¼ teaspoon black pepper
3 tablespoons minced red onion

Whisk together all ingredients except onion, or put them in a jar and shake. Mix in onion.

Makes 1 cup plus

ABOUT THE HOUSE

Records reveal that the site on which the house stands was purchased by Jacob U. Payne and his partner in May 1849, so it seems reasonable to assume building was begun not long after. We might also assume that the structure was designed by Payne himself, carrying forward the eighteenth-century tradition when gentlemen considered skill in architecture a necessary accomplishment.

A happy result of the house having been built at mid-century is that its decoration and style, so admired today, is more restrained than that seen in houses of later vintage when exuberance became the vogue and simplicity was eclipsed. Indeed, it is so perfect an example of dignified Greek Revival style that it has been cited in practically all important studies of the City of Lafayette, as this part of New Orleans was called in 1850.

The house remained in the Payne family until 1935, when it was sold to Mr. and Mrs. William Bradish Forsyth. Their decendants still occupy it as this century draws to a close.

The Forsyth family has done considerable restoration during their tenure, but always under the watchful guidance of respected architectural authorities such as Richard Koch and Samuel Wilson, Jr., whose reputations are rooted not only in their commitment to preservation, but their intimate and sensitive knowledge of classic New Orleans architecture.

One sad occurrence of national historical significance is worth noting. Jefferson Davis, the former president of the Confederacy, died here in a ground-floor bedroom on December 6, 1889. Davis, an intimate friend of the Paynes and their relatives, was taken ill at "Beauvoir," his home on the Mississippi Gulf Coast and brought by ambulance to the house. A marker memorializing the event stands just at the front entrance to the grounds.

Pear and Chili Chutney

Great with any kind of chicken.

2½ pounds firm pears, peeled and chopped
1 cup chopped white onion
3 tablespoons seeded and minced jalapeño pepper
2 Anaheim peppers, roasted, skinned, seeded, and
   chopped coarse
2 red bell peppers, roasted, skinned, seeded, and chopped
   coarse
1½ cups apple cider vinegar
¾ cup *each* light and dark brown sugar, tightly packed
2 teaspoons turmeric
1½ teaspoons minced fresh ginger
1 tablespoon honey
1 tablespoon soy sauce
½ teaspoon salt
1½ teaspoons dry mustard
2 teaspoons cornstarch
2 teaspoons water

Place all ingredients, except cornstarch and water, in
a nonreactive saucepan over medium-high heat.
Dissolve cornstarch in the water and stir in. Bring to
a boil and turn down to a simmer. Cook for about
15 minutes. If pears begins to break apart, remove
from heat sooner.

Cool and refrigerate in covered jars. May be stored
for up to 2 weeks.

Makes 1½ to 2 quarts

Opposite: *The double gallery.* **Below:** *Payne-Strachan house.*

Focaccia Rounds

*This dough may be frozen. If you do so,
divide dough into amounts to make individual rounds
and freeze them separately wrapped.*

½ cup warm water, about 110 degrees
1 package active dry yeast
Pinch of sugar
3 ¾ cups flour
6 medium garlic cloves, peeled
½ cup dry white wine
¼ cup olive oil
1 cup milk
1 teaspoon salt
2 teaspoons minced fresh oregano
2 teaspoons minced fresh basil

Place the water in a small bowl and dissolve the
yeast and sugar. Stir in ¾ cup of flour. Set aside for
45 minutes to 1 hour.

Combine garlic, white wine, and olive oil in a small
saucepan. Cover with the lid slightly ajar (mixture
spatters) and cook over medium heat until garlic is
soft, about 10 minutes. Allow to cool. Drain off and
reserve liquid. Mash garlic with a fork.

In a large mixing bowl, mix milk, salt, oregano,
basil, reserved mashed garlic, and 1 tablespoon of the
garlic oil. Stir in yeast mixture. Mix in enough of the
remaining 3 cups of flour to make a sticky but
kneadable dough. Turn out onto a floured surface
and knead lightly until elastic, 3 to 4 minutes,
sprinkling with a little extra flour if necessary (the
dough should be slightly sticky). Form into a ball
and place in an oiled bowl. Cover with plastic wrap
and allow to rise at least 45 minutes, until doubled
in bulk.

Put a pizza stone in the oven and preheat oven to
475 degrees.

Break off 1 or more tennis ball-size pieces of
dough and roll into a 6-or 7-inch round. Make
indentations with your fingertips about an inch
apart all over tops. Sprinkle about 1 teaspoon of the
reserved garlic oil over each, then salt lightly.

Sprinkle the heated pizza stone with cornmeal,
place round(s) on, and bake for 5 to 6 minutes, or
until golden brown.

Makes 6 to 7 rounds

Sun-Dried Tomato Toasts

These are also good with soup.

1 baguette, 12 to 15 inches long, cut into ½-inch rounds
1 ounce sun-dried tomatoes, sliced thin
6 tablespoons olive oil
Freshly ground black pepper to taste
1 tablespoon grated Romano cheese

Preheat oven to 250 degrees.

Place rounds on a baking sheet. Combine tomatoes and oil in a small saucepan and heat over low flame until just hot. Spoon over bread rounds, dividing evenly. Sprinkle with pepper and then cheese. Bake in a preheated oven for about 8 minutes until dried out slightly.

Makes several dozen

Lora Brody Chocolate Cake

Here it is! Dive in.

½ cup water
1⅓ cups sugar
8 ounces unsweetened chocolate, chopped fine
4 ounces bittersweet chocolate, chopped fine
1 cup (2 sticks) unsalted butter, cut into small pieces, at room temperature
5 large eggs, at room temperature
Dark Chocolate Glaze (recipe follows)
White Chocolate Sauce (recipe follows)

Preheat oven to 350 degrees and place rack in the center. Butter a 9-inch cake pan and line bottom with a circle of parchment. Butter this as well.

Mix water with 1 cup of the sugar in a heavy saucepan and bring to a rapid boil over high heat. Boil 2 minutes. Remove from the heat and stir in the chocolate pieces, stirring until completely melted. Stir in the butter until it melts.

Place eggs in a bowl with the remaining sugar and beat with a hand mixer just until sugar dissolves. Add chocolate mixture to the egg-sugar mixture and completely incorporate. Do not overbeat as this can cause air bubbles.

Scrape batter into the prepared pan. Set pan in a

sturdy jelly roll pan, surround with hot water, and bake for 25 to 30 minutes.

Allow cake to cool for 10 minutes. Run a knife around the edge to release the cake. Cover top with plastic wrap and unmold onto a baking sheet. Put a flat plate over the cake and flip it over. Peel off plastic wrap. Glaze with the dark chocolate mixture below. Serve small wedges with White Chocolate Sauce.

Serves 8 to 12

Dark Chocolate Glaze

1 cup heavy cream
10 ounces bittersweet chocolate, cut into small pieces

Scald cream and stir in chocolate pieces. Mix until melted. Allow to cool slightly before pouring over the cake.

White Chocolate Sauce

1 cup heavy cream
9 ounces good-quality white chocolate, cut into small pieces
½ cup Drambuie

Scald cream. Off the heat, stir in chocolate. Stir until melted. Stir in Drambuie.

Above: *A collection of snuffboxes.* **Opposite top:** *Lora Brody Chocolate Cake.* **Opposite bottom:** *Staffordshire figures.*

A SPORTSMAN'S SUPPER

Short-Favrot House

Roast Duck with Blackberry Sauce

Roasted Potatoes

Sautéed Cabbage

Fresh Mango Chutney

Mixed Salad with Red Wine Vinaigrette

Bananas Foster Shortcake

Spottswood Cabernet Sauvignon,
Napa 1988

For years now there has been a slogan on Louisiana automobile license plates that reads simply "Sportsman's Paradise." Unlike many such boosterisms, this one actually proves to be true if you enjoy fishing and hunting. The state's watery landscape and Gulf coastline nourish a great variety of fish and its piney woods, swamps, and marshlands shelter squirrels, rabbits, deer, doves, and quail as well as more exotic creatures like possum, muskrats, and alligators. And, during the season, skies and marshes are crowded with wild ducks. Wild duck isn't available on menus in the city restaurants, but farm-raised ducks have long been a popular entrée — so city folk don't have to wait for hunting season or the generosity of a hunter friend to get their duck fix. ∾ Of course, another great favorite is fruit of the blackberry family, which thrives in this climate. Some, like the dewberry, are small and sweet, while others grow large. ∾ In this menu we decided to cover both bases by having crispy roast duck with a sauce that contains a hint of blackberry. Accompaniments are roasted potatoes and sautéed cabbage — and just for the heck of it, a flavorful fresh mango chutney. ∾ The meal closes with Bananas Foster Shortcake. Banana desserts have always been part of the cuisine here and none is more famous than Bananas Foster. This shortcake is a variation on that immensely pleasing original.

Opposite: *Roast Duck with Blackberry Sauce, Roasted Potatoes, and Sautéed Cabbage.*

Roast Duck with Blackberry Sauce

This may be done partially in advance —
say, the morning of the day of the dinner —
and finished later to serve.

3 ducks, 4 to 4½ pounds each
¼ cup salt
2 tablespoons black pepper
Blackberry Sauce (recipe follows)

Rinse ducks well with cold water and allow to sit in
a bowl with the cold tap water running slowly over
them for about 20 minutes to further rinse away any
blood. Dry with paper towels. Mix salt and pepper
together and rub all ducks inside and out with it.
Place ducks on a tray, uncovered, in the refrigerator
for several hours or overnight (this helps dry out the
skin).

Preheat oven to 325 degrees.

Place ducks on a roasting rack and bake 40
minutes. Turn heat up to 400 and cook for another
10 to 15 minutes to brown nicely. Remove and
allow to cool. Split the ducks, bone them, and cut
into serving pieces. (You may prepare to this point
and refrigerate for final roasting later.)

To finish, put duck pieces, skin side up, in a
roasting pan and bake at 400 degrees 10 to 15
minutes, until skin is crisp.

Serve with the Blackberry Sauce.

Serves 6

Blackberry Sauce

Make this while the ducks are baking, so it will
be ready to glaze them when they come out of the oven.

1 cup blackberries
1 cup port
2½ cups rich stock (*demi-glace*)
1 teaspoon salt (optional)
½ teaspoon white pepper (optional)

Bring blackberries and port to boil in a nonreactive
saucepan over high heat. Continue at a rolling boil
until reduced by half, 10 to 12 minutes. Add stock
and bring again to a boil. Strain, season, and serve
with the heated duck.

ABOUT THE HOUSE

One of the most striking things about this magnificent house is its sheer size. Typical of the period, the ground floor has two connecting parlors, front and back; not so typical is that they measure forty-three by twenty-six feet. Also untypical is that the back parlor extends into the side yard and ends in a curved bay with an ironwork gallery. This extension so pleased a later owner that he added another one, also with a bay and gallery, to what was already a generously scaled dining room.

The house was built for Colonel Robert Henry Short, a Kentuckian, and its cost was as large as its rooms by standards of its day — a cool $23,750 1859 dollars. The architect was Henry Howard, who opted to work in the Italianate style that was gaining in favor. Although Short's house was asymmetrical, its interior hewed to classic Greek Revival in woodwork and ornamentation, with elaborately carved doors and window frames, and decorated plaster cornices and ceiling medallions. Ornamentation on the exterior is dominated by the fine iron grillwork so typical of New Orleans. And a fence surrounding the property is of the famous cornstalk and morning glory pattern.

As time passed, alterations such as the addition to the dining room were made, but the place has mercifully escaped the sort of voguish renovations that many others of its era fell prey to. So what we are privileged to see today is very much what must have so pleased Colonel Short to gaze upon when his great house was first completed.

Opposite: *Window detail.* Below: *Short-Favrot house.*

Above: *Collection of corn majolica.* **Below left:** *Detail of the cornstalk and morning glory fence.* **Below right:** *Mixed Salad with Red Wine Vinaigrette.* **Opposite:** *Detail of acanthus column.*

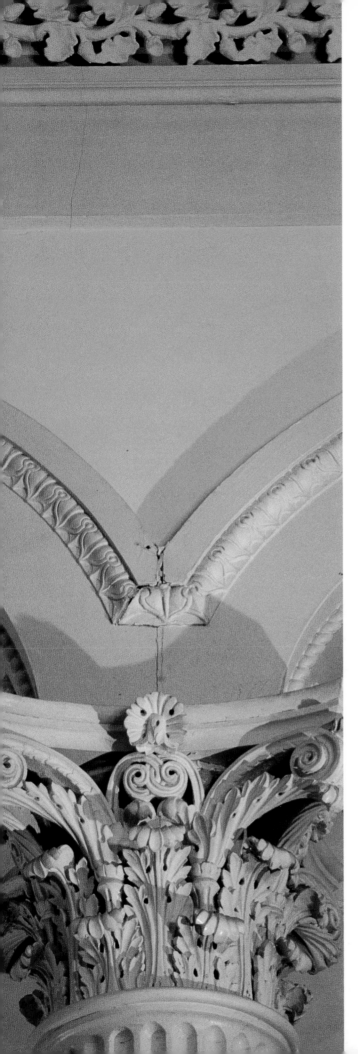

Roasted Potatoes

These are a perfect foil for the duck and cabbage.

2 pounds new red potatoes of approximately the same
    size, quartered but unpeeled
2 tablespoons unsalted butter
1 tablespoon minced garlic
1 teaspoon salt
½ teaspoon white pepper

Preheat oven to 375 degrees.

   Cover potatoes with salted water and bring to a
simmer; cook until just tender, about 12 minutes
(boiling the potatoes rapidly will dislodge the skin).
Drain. In a large ovenproof skillet over medium-high
heat, sauté the potatoes in the butter for about
6 minutes, turning carefully. Sprinkle with the garlic
and toss.

   Place in the oven and roast until nicely browned,
about 12 to 15 minutes. Toss with the salt and
pepper.

Serves 6

Sautéed Cabbage

*This is traditionally sautéed in bacon fat, but you
may use any combination of fat, butter, margarine,
or oil. Of course, you may also just steam the cabbage
and toss it with a little butter and a squeeze of lemon.*

2 tablespoons bacon fat
4 cups thinly shredded green cabbage
1 teaspoon salt
½ teaspoon white pepper

Heat fat in a large skillet over medium heat. Add
cabbage and cook, stirring occasionally, for 12 to
15 minutes until tender. Do not let it brown or
overcook.

   Season with salt and pepper.

Serves 6

Fresh Mango Chutney

You may substitute other fruits in this basic recipe.
If the fruit has firmer flesh, blanch it first.

1 cup sugar
¾ cup sherry vinegar
1 medium white onion, cut into thin julienne strips
2 tablespoons unsalted butter
1 cup sun-dried cherries (see Note)
1 cup diced mango

In a nonreactive saucepan over medium heat, simmer sugar and sherry vinegar until it starts to darken and becomes syrupy, about 15 minutes.

Meanwhile, sauté onion in the butter over medium-high heat until golden and caramelized, about 10 to 12 minutes. Remove from the heat and combine with the syrup. Stir in cherries and mango. Serve warm.

Makes about 2½ cups

Note: If these aren't available in your local specialty market, contact American Spoon Foods at (800) 222-5886.

Mixed Salad with Red Wine Vinaigrette

Use any combination of mixed greens here.

1 tablespoon Dijon-style mustard
¼ cup red wine vinegar
¾ cup olive oil
1 teaspoon minced parsley
1 teaspoon salt
¼ teaspoon white pepper
1 cup peeled, seeded, and coarsely chopped ripe tomato
½ cup sliced mushrooms
6 endive leaves, chopped coarse
6 radicchio leaves, torn into bits
12 small leaves of curly leaf lettuce, torn into bits

Whisk together the mustard, vinegar, and olive oil. Stir in parsley, salt, and pepper. Set aside.

Toss all other ingredients together and add enough vinaigrette to coat lettuce leaves.

Serves 6

Bananas Foster Shortcake

Anyone who likes bananas will love this.

2½ cups flour
2 teaspoons baking soda
¾ teaspoon salt
¾ cup (1½ sticks) unsalted butter, cut into pieces and chilled
1 cup banana puree
4½ cups heavy cream
2½ cups dark brown sugar, tightly packed
2 tablespoons granulated sugar
2½ tablespoons dark rum
2½ tablespoons banana liqueur
5 bananas, peeled and cut into ¾-inch rounds

Preheat the oven to 400 degrees.

Sift together into a mixing bowl the flour, baking soda, and salt. Cut in the cold butter until mixture resembles coarse meal. Lightly stir in banana puree to make a damp dough. Turn out onto a floured surface and roll or pat to 1 inch thick. Cut into 2½- or 3-inch circles with a floured cutter. Place on an ungreased cookie sheet and bake until golden, about 30 minutes.

Combine 2½ cups cream and the brown sugar in a heavy saucepan. Cook over moderate heat, stirring constantly, until slightly thickened, about 10 to 12 minutes. Do not scorch. Allow to cool about 10 minutes.

Meanwhile, whip the balance of the cream and the granulated sugar together until soft peaks are formed.

To assemble, stir rum, banana liqueur, and sliced bananas into the warm sauce. Split the biscuits and place on individual plates. Spoon banana-sauce mixture onto biscuits and top with whipped cream.

Serves 6

Above: *Bananas Foster Shortcake.* **Below left:** *A game table in the library.* **Below right:** *A comfortable corner.*

A New Orleans Chicken Dinner

Westervelt House

Creole Tomatoes with
Café Dressing

Garlic Chicken

Red Bean Succotash

Sweet Potato Cakes

White Chocolate Bread Pudding

Chalone Chardonnay 1990

I was born in Louisiana so I guess it's okay for me to say that Creole tomatoes are the best in the world. Often they are eaten with nothing more to enhance them than a little salt and a grind of pepper. But for those of you who like more zip, we've included a café dressing. Regardless of your preference, they're a pretty nifty way to begin *any* meal. ∿ After the tomatoes, there is pungent garlic chicken, not new, but delicious — served with a local version of succotash. And how about sweet potato cakes? Frankly, I'm keen on sweet potatoes in almost any form. If you share even a small part of my enthusiasm for this vegetable, you'll be delighted with these cakes. They're baked instead of fried, making them easier to prepare than the usual potato cakes — and, if you care, lower in calories. ∿ The dessert, white chocolate bread pudding, will speak (volumes) for itself. It seems every time I come back to New Orleans they have thought of another way to serve bread pudding. Thank heaven.

Left: *Creole Tomatoes with Café Dressing.* **Opposite:** *Oriental lamp and teapot.*

Above: *Table set with Garlic Chicken, Red Bean Succotash, and Sweet Potato Cakes.* **Below:** *Dining room.*

Creole Tomatoes with Café Dressing

Southerners sometime sprinkle their tomatoes with just the least bit of sugar along with salt and pepper.

4 medium-large tomatoes, peeled and sliced
1 egg
½ cup olive oil
2 tablespoons Creole mustard (see Note, page 87)
½ teaspoon white wine vinegar
½ teaspoon salt, or to taste
Pinch of white pepper
2 large fresh basil leaves, minced
Melba toast (optional)

Arrange tomato slices on individual plates.

Beat egg lightly with a whisk, then drizzle in olive oil while continuing to whisk. Whisk in mustard, vinegar, salt, and pepper. Stir in basil leaves.

Spoon over tomato and serve with melba toast.

Serves 6

Garlic Chicken

These chickens may be cooked on an oven rotisserie — if you have such a contraption.

1 tablespoon Creole Seasoning (page 109)
2 tablespoons minced garlic
3 small chickens, 2½ to 2¾ pounds each
1 large onion, cut into chunks
2 large celery ribs, cut into large pieces
3 small medium carrots, scraped and cut into large pieces
Garlic Oil for basting (recipe follows)

Preheat oven to 350 degrees.

Mix the seasoning and garlic together and rub chickens with it inside and out. Divide the vegetables into 3 portions and stuff each chicken. Truss and place breast side down on the rack of a roasting pan.

Bake, basting every 10 to 15 minutes with garlic oil, until juices run clear when thigh is pierced with the point of a knife, about 1 hour and 10 minutes.

Let rest a few minutes before cutting into serving pieces with poultry shears.

Serves 6 to 8

Garlic Oil

This would be great to use for a sharp vinaigrette.

4 large garlic cloves, minced
1 cup olive oil

Put the garlic and oil together in a jar. Shake well, then allow to sit for several hours before using. This will keep in the refrigerator for two weeks or so.

Red Bean Succotash

As you probably already know, red beans are enormously popular here, so it's not surprising to find them in this version of succotash.

½ pound dried red beans
1 large bay leaf
2 tablespoons olive oil
½ medium red onion, diced
½ large green bell pepper, diced
½ cup fresh corn kernels
¾ cup ½-inch rounds of okra
1 medium ripe tomato, peeled, seeded, and diced
¾ teaspoon salt
¼ teaspoon pepper
Pinch of cayenne

Soak red beans overnight. Pour out water and cover beans with about 2 inches of water. Add bay leaf and bring quickly to a boil. Turn heat down to a simmer and cook until just done but not mushy, about 1 hour. Discard the bay leaf and set the beans aside to cool in the liquid.

Heat oil in a medium skillet over medium heat, and sauté onion and peppers until wilted, about 5 minutes. Stir in corn and okra. Cook another minute or two, stirring occasionally. Toss in tomato and remove from the heat. Drain beans and put into a large bowl. Toss in other vegetables and season with salt and pepper.

Serves 6

ABOUT THE HOUSE

In the early part of the nineteenth century when people started moving uptown from the French Quarter, the area on the other side of Canal Street was made up, more or less, of three villages in various stages of evolvement: Lafayette City, which became the Garden District; Faubourg Bouligny, which wound up being called Jefferson City; and Carrolton, which kept its name.

Faubourg Bouligny took its name from Louis Faubourg, who in 1829 attempted to start a sugar plantation there. His scheme soon began to falter, and he was forced to sell half of the plantation to raise capital. Later, a hurricane struck, destroying most of what he had managed to build. Close on the heels of this misfortune was a cholera epidemic that killed most of his slaves. By 1834, Bouligny was out of business. Messrs. Millaudon and Kohn bought Bouligny out and began development of the area in earnest; by 1850 it had become Jefferson City.

There was a racetrack known as Crescent Green in Bouligny, and what is now Westervelt House is thought to have been the home of a horse trainer. The structure was typical of the sort of modest houses that started to spring up in the area. Built of cypress, the older parts of the house are put together with pegs instead of nails. A simple plan divides the interior with a central hall. On one side are living and dining rooms; on the other, the more private parts of the house. Double-hung windows throughout — many with original hand-blown glass panes still in place — provide excellent cross-ventilation.

Any New Orleans house worth its salt has a few stories attached to it. Westervelt House is no exception, though the story is on the thin side. It seems that someone was rummaging in the attic and found an old log for the Steamer *LaBelle,* which traveled the Mississippi from 1867 to 1872. Plus there were those bits of gossip — unverifiable, of course — that lead us to believe that just possibly Mark Twain could have visited the house.

Sweet Potato Cakes

Don't forget these luscious little cakes
when the holidays roll around. They are a fine way
to serve sweet potatoes.

2 to 2¼ pounds sweet potatoes (2 large or 3 medium)
2 tablespoons unsalted butter
½ teaspoon salt
¼ teaspoon black pepper
3 egg whites
6 tablespoons fresh fine white bread crumbs
3 teaspoons Brownulated sugar

Preheat oven to 350 degrees.

Bake potatoes, unpeeled, until tender, 1 to 1¼ hours. When cool enough to handle, peel and place in a bowl with the butter, salt, and pepper. Mash smooth with a fork or a hand mixer. Stir in egg whites and set aside.

Turn up oven to 400 degrees. Sprinkle bread crumbs in a large heavy ovenproof skillet. Bake for 7 or 8 minutes, until crumbs start to turn dark golden. Remove skillet and quickly drop heaping tablespoons of the potato mixture onto the crumbs, leaving a little space between. You should have about 12 cakes.

Bake for 10 minutes. Remove skillet and turn oven to broil. Using the blade of a knife, lift some of the crumbs from the bottom of the pan and sprinkle over each cake, then sprinkle each with a bit of the Brownulated sugar.

Run under the broiler just long enough to melt the sugar. Allow to rest for 3 to 4 minutes before lifting cakes onto dinner plates with a spatula.

Serves 6

Opposite:
Westervelt House.
Right: *White Chocolate Bread Pudding.*

White Chocolate Bread Pudding

Boy, is this good!

4 ounces New Orleans French Bread (page 27), trimmed
    and cut into ¼-inch thick slices
1½ cups half-and-half
½ cup heavy cream
1 whole egg
4 egg yolks
¼ cup sugar
1½ teaspoons vanilla extract
4 ounces white chocolate, melted
White Chocolate Sauce (recipe follows)
Shavings of dark and milk chocolate (optional)

Preheat oven to 350 degrees. Generously butter six ½-cup custard cups.

Cut trimmed bread slices into strips as wide as the depth of the custard cups. Place on a baking sheet and bake until golden, about 10 minutes. Set aside.

Heat half-and-half and cream over a low flame until hot but not boiling. Beat together the egg, yolks, and sugar. Off the heat, whisk a few tablespoons of the cream mixture into the egg mixture to warm it. Whisk eggs into the cream, then stir in the vanilla.

Scrape melted chocolate into a large bowl and slowly whisk the cream mixture into it.

Line sides of custard cups with the bread, breaking it as necessary. Strain custard into cups and let the bread absorb it. Place cups in an ovenproof pan large enough to hold them comfortably. Add more custard if bread has absorbed most of it. Surround cups with boiling water and bake until set and a knife inserted comes out clean, about 35 to 45 minutes.

This may be served in the cups or unmolded. To unmold, chill thoroughly, covered, at least an hour; loosen edges, and invert onto individual plates.

Serve with White Chocolate Sauce, and shavings of dark and milk chocolate over the top of each if desired.

White Chocolate Sauce

¾ cup heavy cream
4 ounces white chocolate, melted

Heat cream until almost boiling. Whisk it into the melted chocolate until smooth. Refrigerate until ready to use.

Index

OTHER BOOKS BY LEE BAILEY

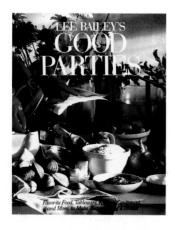

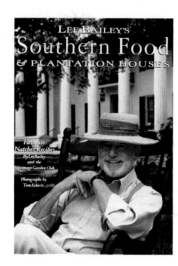
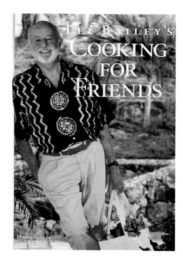
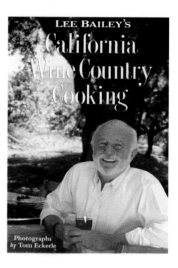

"Lee Bailey understands the headlong pace
of modern life but never quite forgets the hunger
for what was best of our past."
Food & Wine